THE POLITICS OF
ACCOMMODATION

Pluralism and Democracy in the Netherlands

Second Edition, Revised

THE POLITICS OF ACCOMMODATION

PLURALISM AND DEMOCRACY IN THE NETHERLANDS

by Arend Lijphart

UNIVERSITY OF CALIFORNIA PRESS
Berkeley, Los Angeles, London

University of California Press
Berkeley and Los Angeles, California
University of California Press, Ltd.
London, England
Copyright © 1968, by
The Regents of the University of California
Second Edition, 1975
First Paperback Edition, 1975
ISBN: 0–520–02900–3 (paper-bound)
0–520–02918–6 (cloth-bound)
Library of Congress Catalog Card Number: 68–11667
Printed in the United States of America

For Eva

PREFACE TO
THE SECOND EDITION

When I completed the first edition of *The Politics of Accommodation* in 1967, there were already many signs that Dutch politics was changing in a number of important respects. Therefore, I included a chapter called "Dutch Politics in Transition," in which I called attention to the fact that in the 1960's the social cleavages had gradually become less deep and less relevant to the political process, that popular deference and allegiance to the leadership of the religious-ideological blocs was declining, and that elite control appeared to become less firm and confident. In particular, I pointed out that the support for the major parties that together managed the system of accommodation was lower in the 1967 parliamentary elections than ever before—I called this a "clear warning" to the political leaders—and I characterized the year 1966 with its turbulent events that were to a large extent provoked by errors of leadership as "not a year of pride for the politics of accommodation." I also emphasized, however, that it was my intention to analyze the general pattern of Dutch politics as it had operated since 1917 rather than to focus on the 1960s, and that if the latter objective had been consistently pursued, most of the statements would have had to be amended with the qualifying remark, "but the situation may now be changing."

It is now clear that the developments of the mid-1960's were merely the beginning of rapid and far-reaching changes that challenged the very foundations of the politics of accommodation. In fact, with the advantage of hindsight, I now think that the politics of accommodation in the Netherlands came to an end around 1967. The revolutionary changes since then are analyzed in this second edition in a new Chapter X, "The Breakdown of the Politics of Accommodation," which replaces the discussion in the old chapter on "Dutch Politics in Transition." The other chapters are reprinted without change but should now, for the most part, be read in the past tense.

Although for the Netherlands the politics of accommodation has largely become history, it retains its theoretical value as a source of constructive amendments to pluralist theory, its empirical value as an explanation of the pattern of Dutch democracy in the 1917–1967 period, and its practical value as a normative model that is more appropriate than the pluralistic model for the world's many highly divided societies aspiring to democratic rule. Finally, as I shall attempt to show in Chapter X, the recent upheavals in Dutch politics can be understood only in terms of the tensions that were inherent in the politics of accommodation.

Leyden, The Netherlands   A.L.
June 1974

ACKNOWLEDGMENTS

This book has benefited from the assistance given by many people. Earlier drafts of the main thesis were presented at the Center for the Comparative Study of Political Development at the University of Chicago in November 1965, at the Western Complex Societies Colloquium at the University of California, Berkeley, in May 1966, and at the joint meeting of the Smaller European Democracies group and the Committee on Comparative Politics of the Social Science Research Council at Stanford in February 1967. I am deeply grateful to the participants in these colloquia for their patience in listening to me and their many valuable suggestions. I am particularly indebted to Hans Daalder of Leyden University, Johan Goudsblom of the Municipal University of Amsterdam, Val Lorwin of the University of Oregon, Richard Rose of the University of Strathclyde, Glasgow, and John P. Windmuller of Cornell University, for submitting the first draft of the manuscript to a rigorous and detailed critique, and to Ernst B. Haas of the University of California, Berkeley, whose insightful criticisms have greatly strengthened the theoretical framework of the book. I am also grateful for the advice of Gabriel A. Almond and Sidney Verba of Stanford University, Seymour Martin Lipset of Harvard University, Leonard Binder, Grant McConnell, Duncan MacRae, Jr., and Aristide R. Zolberg of the University of Chicago, and my colleagues Giuseppe di Palma, Richard Herr, William Kornhauser, Leslie Lipson, Andrew McFarland, Michael Rogin, Peter W. Sperlich, and Aaron Wildavsky of the University of California, Berkeley.

In the Netherlands, my conversations with both theorists and practitioners of politics have been very useful. I would like to express my appreciation to W. F. de Gaay Fortman, H. van Riel, and J. In 't Veld, members of the First Chamber of the States-General, P. Baehr, M. J. Brouwer, H. Daudt, and G. H. Scholten of the Municipal University of Amsterdam, Jonkheer G. van Benthem van den Bergh of Leyden University, B. V. A. Röling of Groningen University, and O. Janssen of Nijmegen University. The public opinion survey was conducted by the Netherlands Foundation for Statistics in The Hague. I am grateful for the advice of R. Sorgdrager, J. M. van Tulder, and T. Veldman of the Foundation, and J. Haverkamp and H. Lange of the Netherlands Institute of Public Opinion.

This study would not have been possible without the generous financial support provided by the Social Science Research Council in New York, the Institute of International Studies in Berkeley, the Faculty Fellowship program of the University of California, and the Department of Political Science in Berkeley. The public opinion survey in the Netherlands was financed jointly by the Social Science Research Council and the Institute of International Studies. I gratefully acknowledge their contribution.

Jan van Asselt of McPherson College helped me with the sensitive job of translating into Dutch the questions from the *Civic Culture* questionnaire used in the survey. The translations of the passages quoted from Dutch sources are my own.

I should also like to acknowledge with gratitude the permissions to reprint copyrighted materials in my tables, granted by the University of Illinois Press (Tables 1 and 2), the Netherlands Institute of Public Opinion (Tables 21 and 28), Princeton University Press (the data on the United States, the United Kingdom, Germany, and Italy in Tables 24 and 25).

Finally I am indebted to Mrs. Kathleen Wilson for her efficient secretarial work.

For all errors of commission and omission in description and interpretation, I bear sole responsibility.

Berkeley, California   A.L.

CONTENTS

TABLES

Contents

FIGURES

Chapter I
PLURALISM AND DEMOCRACY

The political system of the Netherlands presents a paradox to the social scientist. On the one hand, it is characterized by an extraordinary degree of social cleavage. Deep religious and class divisions separate distinct, isolated, and self-contained population groups. Social communication across class and religious boundary lines is minimal. Each group has its own ideology and its own political organizations: political parties, labor unions, employers' associations, farmers' groups, newspapers, radio and television organizations, and schools—from kindergarten to university. Such a socially and ideologically fragmented system would appear to be highly conducive to dissension and antagonism instead of consensus and cooperation, to ideological tension and extremism instead of pragmatism and moderation, and to governmental immobil-

high Cleavage

ism alternating with revolutionary upsets rather than evolutionary change.

On the other hand, Holland is also one of the most notable examples of a successful democracy. The social and ideological fragmentation of the Dutch people has not been an insurmountable obstacle to the development and firm persistence of a stable, effective, and legitimate parliamentary democracy which has served the people well and which has by and large enjoyed their active support or acquiescence. The present study will attempt to explain this paradox.

The deviant case of Dutch politics has considerable theoretical significance because of the light it can throw on the social conditions of stable and effective democracy. Pluralist theory, especially "sociological" pluralist theory,[1] expounds important propositions on the relationship between social structure and political behavior in a democracy.

[1] The term "pluralism" has many meanings. The kind of pluralist theory which is the concern of this study and which will be discussed in greater detail in this chapter, may be called "sociological" pluralist theory. It focuses on the relationship between social conditions and political behavior. In contrast, what might be termed "political" pluralist theory is primarily concerned with the distribution of political power. As an alternative to the stratification approach to the study of political power, it emphasizes that many separate elites, rather than a single power elite, exert influence in many different problem areas. See Nelson W. Polsby, *Community Power and Political Theory* (New Haven: Yale University Press, 1963), esp. chap. 6; also Robert A. Dahl, *Who Governs? Democracy and Power in an American City* (New Haven: Yale University Press, 1961). Finally, "legal" pluralist theory is normative rather than empirical. In the words of Harold J. Laski, its leading advocate, legal pluralists find the monistic notion of the state as a "hierarchical structure in which power is, for ultimate purposes, collected at a single centre . . . both administratively incomplete and ethically inadequate." The remedy prescribed is decentralization, particularly along functional lines, and corporate representation. See Laski's "The Pluralistic State," in *The Foundations of Sovereignty and Other Essays* (New York: Harcourt, Brace, 1921), p. 240. See also Kung Chuan Hsiao, *Political Pluralism: A Study in Contemporary Political Theory* (New York: Harcourt, Brace, 1927).

For analytical purposes, we can identify three of these propositions.

The first and simplest pluralist proposition is the usually unspoken but implicit assumption that viable democratic government faces grave obstacles in so-called "plural societies," that is, societies with clearly discernible racial, linguistic, and religious differences. Aristotle summarizes this idea succinctly: "A state aims at being, as far as it can be, a society composed of equals and peers."[2] Leslie Lipson prefaces his discussion of linguistic and religious differences with a general statement concerning the consequences of social homogeneity and heterogeneity: "Anything basic . . . that unites human beings makes agreement easier and fosters subjectively that awareness of belonging together which students of politics call a consensus. Conversely, whatever divides men socially groups them in separate camps. Then it is usually but a short step from separation to opposition."[3] Herman Finer contrasts the beneficial "unifying, pacifying effect of the homogeneity of the British population on its government" with the distinctly unfavorable situation in the French nation which "is internally divided in religion, attachment to historic ideals, economic interests, and visions of humanity."[4]

Agreement on the proposition that social heterogeneity tends to be detrimental to stable democratic government is widespread, but there are dissenting voices. In particular, the liberal philosophy of democratic politics emphasizes the benefits of diversity. Social heterogeneity and dissension may endanger the stable democratic order, but, in the words of Reinhard Bendix, "too much agreement is a hazard as

[2] Aristotle, *Politics*, trans. Ernest Barker (New York and London: Oxford University Press, 1958), p. 181.

[3] Leslie Lipson, *The Democratic Civilization* (New York: Oxford University Press, 1964), p. 120

[4] Herman Finer, *Governments of Greater European Powers* (New York: Henry Holt, 1956), pp. 17, 271.

well."⁵ This view is clearly stated by liberalism's eloquent
spokesman John Stuart Mill. His description of social
changes in nineteenth-century England would not have
worried Aristotle: "The circumstances which surround
different classes and individuals, and shape their characters,
are daily becoming more assimilated. Formerly, different
ranks, different neighborhoods, different trades and profes-
sions lived in what might be called different worlds; at
present, to a great degree in the same."⁶ But Mill believed,
of course, that this trend toward conformity was a liability
rather than an asset to a liberal democracy.

The two views epitomized by Mill and Aristotle are
compatible, however. It would be inaccurate to contrast the
former as an advocate of heterogeneity with the latter as
advocate of homogeneity. The difference is merely one of
degree. [A democracy providing stability and individual
freedom must have both a minimum of social homogeneity
and a minimum of heterogeneity] On this formulation of the
relationship between social differences and viable democracy
both parties can agree.⁷ Unfortunately, this pluralist proposition is rather vague and leaves the most important questions
unanswered: What constitutes a minimum of homogeneity
or heterogeneity? How far are the two minima apart on the
homogeneity-heterogeneity continuum? With how many
and how deep differences can a democracy exist before
approaching the danger zone of dissension, revolt, and
dissolution?

⁵ Reinhard Bendix, *Nation-Building and Citizenship: Studies of
Our Changing Social Order* (New York: John Wiley, 1964), p. 22.
⁶ John Stuart Mill, *On Liberty*, ed. Currin V. Shields (New York:
The Liberal Arts Press, 1956), p. 89.
⁷ For instance, Mill recognized that the benefits of social diversity
depend on the existence of a fundamental consensus. A political system can successfully pass through turbulent times, only if "however
important the interests about which men fall out, the conflict did not
affect the fundamental principles of the system of social union which
happened to exist." John Stuart Mill, "Coleridge," in F. R. Leavis,
ed., *Mill on Bentham and Coleridge* (London: Chatto & Windus,
1962), p. 123.

The second pluralist proposition attaches great significance to the existence of many secondary groups. The first
type of pluralism was defined as social heterogeneity, and
the second type can be defined as *organized* social heterogeneity. Alexis de Tocqueville, the acknowledged spiritual
father of this school of thought, presents the main thesis. He
argues that a multiplicity of secondary groups perform two
vital functions in a democracy. In the first place, they contribute to the dispersion of power and thereby check and
balance governmental power. At the same time they prevent
a dangerous atomization of society and alienation of the
individual.[8] By forming a buffer that insulates elites and
nonelites from encroachment by each other, to borrow
William Kornhauser's phraseology,[9] secondary groups help
preserve moderation and individual freedom.

A radically different view of the effects of the second type
of pluralism is that of Rousseau. He believes that "partial
societies" are a threat to democracy because they tend to
distort the general will.[10] In his view, secondary groups are
not buffers guarding individual liberty but weapons that
large groups may use to dominate and suppress minorities,
with potentially divisive consequences. This is also Madison's main worry in the Tenth Federalist Paper. He speaks
of the "mischiefs of faction" and the particular danger of the
"superior force of an interested and overbearing majority."[11]

As the difference between Aristotle and Mill is only one
of degree, so, similarly, the disagreement between De
Tocqueville and the Rousseau-Madison position can be
largely reconciled. Neither Rousseau nor Madison is an

[8] Alexis de Tocqueville, *Democracy in America*, esp. Book 4,
chap. 7. The first of De Tocqueville's propositions belongs to "political" rather than "sociological" pluralist theory (see above, n. 1).

[9] William Kornhauser, *The Politics of Mass Society* (New York:
The Free Press of Glencoe, 1959), chap. 3.

[10] Jean Jacques Rousseau, *The Social Contract*, trans. G. D. H.
Cole (New York: E. P. Dutton, 1950), esp. Book 2, chap. 3.

[11] James Madison, *The Federalist* (New York: The Modern Library, n.d.), pp. 54–55.

absolute enemy of secondary groups. Although Rousseau
holds that it is "essential . . . that there should be no partial
society within the State . . . ," he also considers, as a rather
reluctant afterthought, the next best situation: "But if there
are partial societies, it is best to have as many as possible
and to prevent them from being unequal."[12] Madison goes
further. Though agreeing with Rousseau on the theoretical
desirability of a society without factions, the tenor of his argument is less negative. He believes that the formation of
factions is inevitable, and rejects the notion of forcible sup-
pression. His second best, but enthusiastically endorsed, solution is similar to Rousseau's reluctant prescription of increasing the number of factions as much as possible: "A
greater variety of parties and interests . . . make it less probable that a majority of the whole will have a common motive
to invade the rights of other citizens."[13]

Rousseau and Madison contribute important elements to
the second pluralist proposition. In addition to conceding
the desirability of many secondary groups, they specify that
these should be small—not approaching majority status—
and substantially equal in size. Still, the second pluralist
proposition is not notably more precise than the first. What
degree of pluralism is required to maintain democracy? How
is pluralism measured—by the number of associations or the
incidence of individual affiliation?[14] Furthermore, this pluralist thesis, in its concern with the public good and the preservation of individual freedom pays scant attention to the
requirements of social integration and political cohesion. It
assumes that the interplay of intermediate associations occurs
within a basically consensual society, and that their great

[12] Rousseau, p. 27.

[13] Madison, p. 61. Madison's argument also differs from Rousseau's in that his "factions" are not exclusively organized groups. To
the extent that he emphasizes unorganized groups of people "actuated
by some common impulse of passion, or of interest," he should be
classified among the first group of pluralist writers.

[14] See Kornhauser, pp. 79–81.

number precludes exclusive loyalties and thus tempers potentially explosive differences. This is not necessarily so in all cases. There may be many groups and a high incidence of affiliation but little or no participation and social communication across basic cleavages, with most group activity taking place within each isolated and self-contained segment of the population: a situation conducive to sharp disagreements, extremist behavior, and the possibility of disintegration.

The third pluralist proposition addresses itself to this problem. An elaboration and refinement of the second proposition, it attempts to take into account the prerequisites of both individual freedom and political cohesion. The crucial element added by the third pluralist proposition is the idea of crosscutting affiliations. Seymour M. Lipset states: "The available evidence suggests that the chances for stable democracy are enhanced to the extent that groups and individuals have a number of crosscutting, politically relevant affiliations. To the degree that a significant proportion of the population is pulled among conflicting forces, its members have an interest in reducing the intensity of political conflict."[15] Mutually reinforcing cleavages have the opposite effect. Kornhauser contrasts "cross-cutting solidarities" and a "plurality of groups that are both independent and *noninclusive*" both of which are conducive to stable democracy, with a plurality of "*inclusive*" intermediate groups which, in extreme form, characterize medieval communal society.[16]

This proposition is widely accepted and applied not only by the pluralists themselves but also by the major authorities on group theory, conflict theory, structural-functional theory, and communication theory. Group theorists, closely akin to the pluralists, endorse the proposition in almost identical terms. Arthur F. Bentley, commenting on the question of whether a "mass grouping" or "all-embracing classification"

[15] Seymour Martin Lipset, *Political Man: The Social Bases of Politics* (Garden City, N.Y.: Doubleday, 1960), pp. 88–89.
[16] Kornhauser, pp. 80–81 (italics added).

exists in modern nations in the form of "classes that enter into the class warfare of socialism," states that

> the observed reactions in our societies are not such as would follow from such a grouping in which the criss-cross had disappeared, and sharply defined outlines were traceable—the war in fact is not to the finish, the socialism that extends itself to large portions of the population is, wherever we know it, a socialism that ends in political compromises. And *compromise—not in the merely logical sense, but in practical life —is the very process itself of the criss-cross groups in action.*[17]

David B. Truman, describing American politics as a "protean complex of crisscrossing relationships,"[18] attributes its stability to the existence of overlapping group memberships. He argues that "in the long run a complex society may experience revolution, degeneration, and decay. If it maintains its stability, however, it may do so in large measure because of the fact of multiple memberships."[19]

The crosscutting cleavages proposition is also endorsed in the writings of conflict theorists. Lewis A. Coser concludes, on the basis of notions suggested by Georg Simmel and Edward A. Ross, that "the multiple group affiliations of individuals make for a multiplicity of conflicts criss-crossing society. Such segmental participation, then, can result in a kind of balancing mechanism, preventing deep cleavages along one axis." Such a pattern, Coser argues, is an important check against a "basic consensual breakdown."[20] Another example is Ralf Dahrendorf who uses three sets of terms for the

[17] Arthur F. Bentley, *The Process of Government: A Study of Social Pressures* (4th ed., Evanston, Ill.: The Principia Press of Illinois, 1955), p. 208 (italics added).

[18] David B. Truman, *The Governmental Process: Political Interests and Public Opinion* (New York: Alfred A. Knopf, 1951), p. 508.

[19] *Ibid.*, p. 168.

[20] Lewis A. Coser, *The Functions of Social Conflict* (Glencoe: The Free Press, 1956), pp. 78–79.

distinction between crosscutting and mutually reinforcing cleavages: he contrasts "pluralism" with "superimposition," "dissociation" with "congruence," and "divergence" with "parallelism."[21]

Structural-functional analysis operates on the basis of assumptions radically different from those of conflict theory,[22] but scholars belonging to both schools of thought agree on the crosscutting cleavages proposition. Talcott Parsons, for instance, endorses it in commenting on the results of American voting studies. He notes the strong relationships between party choice and various social groupings to which the voter belongs, but also emphasizes that these are not rigid and do not coincide—an important protection against the divisive potentialities of cleavage: "The essential fact here is that most structurally important groupings in the society will contain considerable proportions of adherents of *both* parties. To an important degree, therefore, the structural ties that bind them together on nonpolitical bases cut across their political allegiances."[23] Using the concept of political culture, Gabriel A. Almond contrasts the homogeneous cultures of the Anglo-American political systems with the fragmented cultures of countries like France, Germany, and Italy. These countries which have clearly separate "political subcultures" with separate "sub-systems of rôles" (churches, schools, trade unions, parties, press, and so on),

[21] Ralf Dahrendorf, *Class and Class Conflict in Industrial Society* (Stanford: Stanford University Press, 1959), pp. 213–218. See also James S. Coleman's discussion of the third pluralist proposition specifically with regard to religious differences: "Social Cleavage and Religious Conflict," *Journal of Social Issues*, Vol. 12, No. 3 (1956), pp. 44–56.

[22] See Ralf Dahrendorf, "Out of Utopia: Toward a Reorientation of Sociological Analysis," *American Journal of Sociology*, Vol. 64, No. 2 (September 1958), pp. 115–127.

[23] Talcott Parsons, " 'Voting' and the Equilibrium of the American Political System," in Eugene Burdick and Arthur J. Brodbeck, eds., *American Voting Behavior* (Glencoe, Ill.: The Free Press, 1959), p. 102.

are therefore prone to "immobilism" and the possibility of a "Caesaristic breakthrough."[24] In a later work, Almond pursues the same theme when he expresses a preference for "broadly aggregative" parties, "associational interest groups," an autonomous press, and proper boundary maintenance among the different political structures.[25] Here again, mutually reinforcing cleavages are identified with political instability.

Finally, communications theorist Karl W. Deutsch provides another endorsement of the proposition—though not as explicitly as the cited writers. Deutsch argues that integration depends on wide and effective social communication habits, and that, conversely, severe discontinuities in communication and transaction habits lead to disintegration.[26] Integration and stability require links of social communication, and, more specifically, crosscutting links: *"unbroken links*, in terms of social institutions, facilities, and social groups, *connecting* the different classes or regions."[27]

Acceptance and approval of the third pluralist proposition is nearly universal. Even the few ostensible critics do not strike at the heart of the cross-cutting cleavages proposition. Joseph R. Gusfield concentrates his criticism on the second pluralist proposition, and in fact endorses Dahrendorf's thesis: "It is fairly evident that intense social conflicts are maximized under conditions of superimposition [mutually rein-

[24] Gabriel A. Almond, "Comparative Political Systems," *Journal of Politics*, Vol. 18, No. 3 (August 1956), pp. 406–408.

[25] Gabriel A. Almond, "Introduction: A Functional Approach to Comparative Politics," in Gabriel A. Almond and James S. Coleman, eds., *The Politics of the Developing Areas* (Princeton: Princeton University Press, 1960), pp. 3–64. See also Gabriel A. Almond and G. Bingham Powell, Jr., *Comparative Politics: A Developmental Approach* (Boston, Little, Brown, 1966), pp. 110–112, 263–266.

[26] Karl W. Deutsch, *Nationalism and Social Communication: An Inquiry into the Foundations of Nationality* (Cambridge, Mass.: Technology Press, 1953), esp. pp. 70–74.

[27] Karl W. Deutsch, *Political Community at the International Level: Problems of Definition and Measurement* (Garden City, N.Y.: Doubleday, 1954), p. 58 (italics added).

forcing cleavages] and minimized under conditions of linked pluralism [crosscutting cleavages]."[28] Stanley Rothman does not question the moderating effect of overlapping membership but has doubts about the value of this proposition because it does not explain why memberships overlap in one case but not in another. He also calls attention to an important force of moderation which may have greater influence than overlapping affiliations: "a prudent leadership which seems to have a better conception [than the rank and file] of what political and social realities permit."[29] This is a suggestive hypothesis with regard to Dutch politics, and will be discussed at greater length below.

The most thorough critique, by William C. Mitchell, concentrates on Truman's version of the overlapping-membership proposition in the context of American politics. Mitchell carefully dissects it, and criticizes it on both logical and empirical grounds. He does not deny the possibility that cross pressures may lead to political moderation but argues that cross pressures may also have different consequences, such as "compartmentalization" of simultaneously maintained contradictory loyalties or "frustration and nonrational adaptation." He also questions the extent to which cross pressures actually exist in American politics and, consequently, their contribution to the stability of the system. The second critical question Mitchell raises about the explanatory power of the overlapping membership thesis is of particular significance in this case study of Dutch politics, and will be developed more fully later. He points out that even when there is little or no overlap, it may still be possible to achieve political stability: "Groups without overlapping members can also arrive at an equilibrium position, under

[28] Joseph R. Gusfield, "Mass Society and Extremist Politics," *American Sociological Review*, Vol. 27, No. 1 (February 1962), p. 29.
[29] Stanley Rothman, "Systematic Political Theory: Observations on the Group Approach," *American Political Science Review*, Vol. 54, No. 1 (March 1960), esp. pp. 21–25.

certain conditions," according to the classical balance-of-power notion.[30]

Although one finds "widespread use of the overlapping membership theory,"[31] as Sidney Verba puts it without exaggeration, there are a number of important differences between the ideas of the many scholars who are in accord with the general import of the theory, and its specific formulation in terms of overlapping memberships in formally organized groups. In the first place,⌈group affiliation is usually interpreted in the sense of membership in nonassociational as well as in associational groups⌋ Truman emphasizes the importance of overlapping membership in "potential groups," which he defines as "any mutual interest" or "any shared attitude."[32] Dahrendorf also adopts this inclusive meaning when he contrasts crosscutting with coinciding "fronts of conflict,"[33] and Coser, Parsons, Almond, and Deutsch similarly do not restrict their analyses to organized groups. Kornhauser also holds this view when he states, for instance, that crosscutting solidarities "help prevent one line of social cleavage from becoming dominant . . . ; they may be contrasted with situations in which religious and class lines tend to closely correspond, as in France where anti-clericalism is largely a working-class phenomenon."[34] And Lipset consid-

[30] William C. Mitchell, "Interest Group Theory and 'Overlapping Memberships': A Critique" (unpublished paper presented at the annual meeting of the American Political Science Association, 1963), pp. 8, 12. Robert A. Dahl, while calling the overlapping membership hypothesis "ingenious" and "highly plausible," also calls attention to the fact that "nothing except the most fragmentary evidence exists" for it; see his *A Preface to Democratic Theory* (Chicago: University of Chicago Press, 1956), p. 105.

[31] Sidney Verba, "Organizational Membership and Democratic Consensus," *Journal of Politics*, Vol. 27, No. 3 (August 1965), p. 497. Verba's own findings are that "the data do not support the hypotheses, but it would be going too far to say that they refute them" (*ibid.*).

[32] Truman, p. 511.

[33] Dahrendorf, *Class and Class Conflict*, pp. 213–218.

[34] Kornhauser, p. 80.

ers not only overlapping memberships in the narrow sense, but "multiple and politically inconsistent *affiliations, loyalties, and stimuli.*"[35] In short, the third pluralist proposition which was interpreted above as a refinement of the second proposition turns out to be an elaboration of the first one as well. This pattern may be summarized in the following typology:

	Nonassociational groups	Associational groups
Congruent cleavage	I	II
Crosscutting cleavage	III,B	III,A

A second and more drastic modification of the crosscutting cleavages proposition is the one introduced by Bentley and Truman. Truman's concept of potential groups includes not only "potential groups representing separate minority elements" but also the politically more significant "interests or expectations that are so widely held in the society and are so reflected in the behavior of almost all citizens that they are, so to speak, taken for granted." These Truman calls the "rules of the game."[36] Thus the concept of potential groups is stretched to include society as a whole, and a general political consensus is regarded as one kind, indeed the most important kind, of group interest. Only thus, Truman argues, can governmental activity be described as "the product or resultant of interest group activity."[37] Bentley uses the similar concept of "habit background" and explains its importance as follows: "When the struggle proceeds too harshly at any point there will become insistent in the society a group more powerful than either of those in-

[35] Lipset, p. 88 (italics added). See also Robert E. Lane, *Political Life: Why People Get Involved in Politics* (Glencoe, Ill.: The Free Press, 1959), pp. 197–203.

[36] Truman, pp. 511–512. He further equates the "rules of the game" with "systems of belief" or "general ideological consensus" (*ibid.*, p. 512).

[37] *Ibid.*, p. 515.

volved which tends to suppress the extreme and annoying methods of the groups in the primary struggle. It is within the embrace of these great lines of activity that the smaller struggles proceed, and the very word struggle has meaning only with reference to its limitations."[38] This modification of the crosscutting cleavages proposition substantially weakens it. Instead of arguing that crosscutting affiliations and solidarities produce moderation and consensus, Bentley and Truman maintain that a consensus—"rules of the game" or "habit background"—must exist as a precondition for the successful operation of a pluralist political system. This entails a reversal of the causal thrust of the thesis and a considerable reduction of its explanatory power.

A third modification is implicit in almost all versions of the crosscutting cleavages proposition. The usual argument emphasizes the importance of crosspressures on the individual group member, but crosspressures also operate on a different level—the political and social leadership. Verba formulates this aspect of the proposition as follows: "On the elite level, organizational leaders reduce the intensity of their claims on other social groups because of the diversity membership in their organization."[39] Kornhauser recognizes the important effect of overlapping affiliations on the actions and decisions of the elite, rather than those of the rank and file, when he states that "extensive *cross-cutting solidarities* . . . constrain associations [i.e. the *leaders* of the associations] to respect the various affiliations of their members lest they alienate them."[40]

The logic of the third pluralist proposition, thus modified, is most compelling—in the abstract. This makes the concrete test case of Dutch politics doubly interesting and worthy of a thoroughgoing examination. The Dutch case is *prima facie*

[38] Bentley, p. 372.
[39] Verba, p. 469.
[40] Kornhauser, p. 80.

contrary to the crosscutting cleavages proposition.[41] Expressed in the jargon of the cited writers, Dutch politics is characterized by "mutually reinforcing," "superimposed," "congruent," and "parallel" rather than "crosscutting" affiliations and organizational patterns; class and religious cleavages separate self-contained "inclusive" groups with sharply defined "political subcultures"; and there is a multiparty system with considerable "interpenetration" within each sphere among parties, interest groups, and the communication media. But Dutch democracy is eminently stable and effective!

Though the Dutch case clearly appears to be deviant, its analysis in the context of pluralist theory will not lead to the wholesale rejection of the third pluralist proposition. If amended and refined in a number of important respects—along the lines of the three modifications discussed above and the suggestions advanced by Rousseau, Madison, Rothman, and Mitchell—the third pluralist proposition retains much of its validity.[42]

[41] With the important exceptions noted below, pp. 88–94, 118–121, and 189–190.

[42] This study is not a country study in the conventional sense. It is an extended theoretical argument based on a single case of particular significance to pluralist theory. It analyzes only those aspects of Dutch politics, therefore, which are relevant in this context; no attempt is made to provide an exhaustive description of all facets of the political system. Furthermore, it analyzes the general pattern of stable politics developed and maintained during the twentieth century, and does not attempt to focus narrowly on the contemporary state of affairs in the year 1967. Dutch society and politics are not static, of course; the situation after the Second World War differs in many important respects from the interwar period, and in the middle of the 1960's some particularly far-reaching changes appear to be taking place. These will be discussed briefly in Chapter X against the backdrop of the established pattern.

Chapter II

A NATION DIVIDED

RELIGIOUS AND CLASS CLEAVAGES

The two basic cleavages which divide the Dutch population are class and religion. Religious differences are felt deeply and have a long historical background in the Netherlands. At the time of the last decennial census (1960), the religious composition of the population was: Roman Catholics 40.4 per cent, Dutch Reformed (*Nederlands Hervormd*) 28.3 per cent, and various orthodox Reformed (*Gereformeerd*, not to be confused with the Dutch Reformed) groups 9.3 per cent. Other smaller groups, like Mennonites, Lutherans, and Jews, together had 3.6 per cent, and those without religious affiliation 18.4 per cent. The socially relevant cleavages do not neatly coincide with the pattern of formal denominational affiliations, however. The social cleavages present a threefold division into Roman Catholic, orthodox Calvinist, and secular subcultures which are based not only on formal affiliations but also on the de-

gree of religious commitment. In Holland, these three subcultural groups are usually called *zuilen* (literally: pillars,
that is, vertical social groups), and we shall henceforth term
them "blocs."

The Catholic bloc coincides closely with the formal members of the Roman Catholic Church with the exception of
the relatively small group of liberal or only nominal Catholics who belong to the secular bloc.

The orthodox Calvinist bloc consists of the members of
several Protestant churches: (1) the Reformed Church, characterized by strict adherence to orthodox Calvinist doctrines,
which broke away from the too "liberal" Dutch Reformed
Church in the late nineteenth century—it should be emphasized once more that the *Dutch Reformed* Church and the
Reformed Church are *different* churches, in spite of the unfortunately rather confusing similarity of names; (2) a number of smaller, even more fundamentalist Calvinist churches
which are also called "Reformed churches" but which have
a total membership of only slightly more than a third of that
of the main Reformed Church; (3) the orthodox wing of
the Dutch Reformed Church comprising roughly a third of
the membership of that church.

The third bloc which, for lack of a better term, we shall
call the secular bloc, consists of those not belonging to any
church, the majority of Dutch Reformed (the liberal wing
plus those who are only nominal members), the small group
of liberal and nonpracticing Roman Catholics, and most of
the members of the minor dissenting churches.

This threefold division goes back as far as the birth of the
Dutch state and nation in the sixteenth century, and can be
traced to the three forces of Roman Catholicism, Renaissance, and Reformation. The religious dimension of the
Dutch struggle for independence from Spain was the Catholic-Protestant conflict. At the same time, however, the Protestants were split into two feuding groups: the strict Calvinists versus the more liberal Arminians, who were influenced,

like the liberal Erasmians in the Roman Catholic Church, by
the freethinking and tolerant spirit of Renaissance thought.[1]
The three blocs have remained the basic component parts
of the Dutch people.

Each group has its traditional geographical stronghold:
the Catholics in the South, the Calvinists in the Southwest
and center, and the secular bloc in the West and North of the
country. They are not geographically isolated from each
other, however. For instance, the Catholic bloc which is geographically the most concentrated bloc, is well represented
throughout the country. Using the percentages of declared
Roman Catholics in the 1960 census as approximations of
the size of the Catholic bloc in each of the provinces, we
find that almost half of all Dutch Catholics live in the two
southern provinces of North Brabant and Limburg where
they constitute the overwhelming majority of the population
(89.0 and 94.4 per cent respectively). They are only a small
minority in the three northeastern provinces (somewhat less
than 10 per cent), but in the other six provinces, including
the two most heavily populated western provinces, their
percentage remains above 25 per cent. The statistics for the
municipalities reveal a similar picture of religious heterogeneity coupled with a certain degree of geographical concentration—especially in rural areas—at the local level.[2]

In addition to these deep, historically rooted religious
cleavages, Dutch society is also divided by class cleavages.
Class differences in the Netherlands are similar to those in
most complex industrialized societies. There are clearly
identifiable upper middle, lower middle, and lower classes.
It should be noted, however, that the antithesis between

[1] See J. P. Kruijt and Walter Goddijn, "Verzuiling en ontzuiling
als sociologisch proces," in A. N. J. den Hollander, et al., eds., *Drift
en koers: Een halve eeuw sociale verandering in Nederland* (Assen:
Van Gorcum, 1962), pp. 230–231.

[2] Centraal Bureau voor de Statistiek, *13ᵉ Algemene volkstelling,
31 mei 1960: Deel 7. Kerkelijke gezindte, B. Voornaamste cijfers per
gemeente* (Zeist: De Haan, 1963), pp. 26–29.

middle class and lower class in Holland has stronger historical roots than in most other countries. Elsewhere the middle classes usually did not come to power until the dawn of the modern industrial age, but the Dutch bourgeoisie has had predominant power ever since the struggle for independence and the foundation of the Netherlands Republic around the year 1600.

During the past century, objective economic inequalities between classes have gradually decreased, as in most countries of the industrialized West. Still, the Gini Index of Inequality for Holland, based on the 1950 figures of income distribution before taxes, was relatively high (0.431). Of the other Western countries, only West Germany had greater inequality and (in descending order) Denmark, Italy, Sweden, the United States, Canada, Norway, the United Kingdom, New Zealand, and Australia had less inequality.[3] The year 1950, following shortly upon the Second World War and the Indonesian conflict, may have been atypical. However, a similar comparison for 1955 according to a different indicator of inequality—the percentage of the total income earned by the 5 per cent with the highest incomes—also reveals a relatively high degree of inequality in Holland compared with three other countries. The top 5 per cent in Holland had 24 per cent of the total income. The comparable percentages for the United States, England, and Sweden in 1955 were 21, 20, and 17 per cent respectively. The figures for the top 10 per cent in these four countries follow the same rank order: 34 per cent in Holland, 31 per cent in the United States, 29 per cent in England, and 28 per cent in Sweden.[4]

[3] Bruce M. Russett, et al., *World Handbook of Political and Social Indicators* (New Haven: Yale University Press, 1964), p. 245. Holland ranks somewhat lower on the Gini Index of Inequality *after* taxes (*ibid.*, p. 247). See also F. van Heek, "Sociale ongelijkwaardigheid en verticale mobiliteit in de 20ste eeuw: Wijzigingen en continuiteit," in *Drift en Koers*, pp. 149–179.

[4] Centraal Bureau voor de Statistiek, *Statistische en Econometrische Onderzoekingen* (2nd quarter, 1960), p. 54.

It is difficult to assess the relative strength and persistence of class loyalties and class antagonisms in twentieth-century Holland. As Johan Goudsblom points out, "social stratification is seldom made the topic of public discussion" in Holland, and "even sociologists have tended to shun the topic—they have produced many valuable statistical reports bearing on various aspects of socioeconomic status, but so far no attempt has been made at a comprehensive analysis of social classes in contemporary Dutch society." Goudsblom reports that clear instances of social discrimination are rare, and, when they do occur, evoke widespread indignation. On the other hand, "social interaction between the [manual and the nonmanual workers] tends to be limited."[5] David O. Moberg, in an article on religious divisions in the Netherlands, begins with the assertion that "differentiation along socioeconomic lines is quickly apparent to the observer who seeks evidences of it. Social status . . . colors all social relationships."[6]

Comparative survey findings suggest that class feelings are more pronounced in Holland than in most other Western democracies. Strong evidence can be found in the cross-country survey under UNESCO auspices conducted in 1948 in nine different countries. To measure the distinctness of class cleavages two items were included in the questionnaire: (1) The respondents were asked: "If you were asked to use a name for your social class, would you say you belong to the middle class, working class, or upper class?" (2) The interviewers were asked to indicate to which of four socioeconomic groups the respondents belonged. Table 1 gives the correlations between the subjective self-assigned class identifications of the respondents and the "objective" judgment of the interviewers concerning the respondents' status. Assum-

[5] Johan Goudsblom, *Dutch Society* (New York: Random House, 1967), pp. 63, 67.
[6] David O. Moberg, "Social Differentiation in the Netherlands," *Social Forces*, Vol. 39, No. 4 (May 1961), p. 333.

TABLE 1.   INDICES OF CLASS CLEAVAGE
r^2 x 100

Germany	59
Netherlands	50
Mexico	49
Britain	32
Italy	31
Australia	25
France	22
United States	14
Norway	10

NOTE: The measure of correlation is the product-moment coefficient, squared and multiplied by 100.

SOURCE: William Buchanan and Hadley Cantril, *How Nations See Each Other: A Study in Public Opinion* (Urbana: University of Illinois Press, 1953), p. 17.

ing that a high degree of agreement between respondent and interviewer on the former's status indicates the existence of rigid and distinct class lines, high indices of correlation mean rigid and distinct cleavages and low indices mean a loose and indistinct class structure. The Netherlands is in the second place. Together with Germany and Mexico, it is far ahead of the other six countries. Perhaps Holland's real position should be even higher, because there are serious doubts regarding the validity of the index of correlation for Germany. The German questionnaire used almost the same terms for subjective self-assigned as for objective interviewer-assigned class identification instead of the usual A, B, C, D classification used in the other questionnaires. This was bound to raise the German correlation, and casts doubt on its comparability with the other correlations.[7]

[7] Furthermore, it is not clear how the four categories of objective socioeconomic status were derived from the three socioeconomic check boxes on the questionnaire. See Buchanan and Cantril, pp. 152–153. The German sample was restricted to the population of the British Zone of Occupation.

The UNESCO survey also attempted to compare class
and national loyalties. The answers to two questions included
in the questionnaire for this purpose provide additional
strong evidence of the depth of Dutch class cleavages. The
respondents were asked: (1) "Do you feel that you have
anything in common with [own] class people abroad?" (2)
"Do you feel that you have anything in common with [own
nationality] people who are not [own] class?" Table 2 pre-

TABLE 2.   NATIONAL AND CLASS ALLEGIANCE
(In per cent)

Country	Class allegiance	National allegiance
Australia	67	78
Britain	58	67
France	48	63
Germany	30	64
Italy	41	50
Mexico	40	56
Netherlands	61	56
Norway	41	64
United States	42	77

SOURCE: Buchanan and Cantril, p. 18.

sents the percentages replying affirmatively to these two
questions. Three conclusions stand out. The percentage of
Dutchmen feeling class allegiance even across international
boundaries is strikingly high; with 61 per cent, Holland is
again in second place only exceeded by Australia with 67
per cent. The second column is even more striking: The percentage of Dutchmen who feel that they have anything in
common with other classes in their own country is among
the lowest; Holland shares the second-lowest place with
Mexico (56 per cent), Italy being at the very bottom (50
per cent). A comparison of the two columns of figures
shows that in all countries the percentage of national allegiance is greater than that of class allegiance *except in the
Netherlands*; in the other eight countries, national allegiance

exceeds class allegiance by at least 9 percentage points (Britain and Italy) and in two cases (United States and Germany) by as much as 35 and 34 percentage points, but in Holland it is actually 5 points lower.[8]

This deep class cleavage cuts through the Catholic, Calvinist, and secular blocs. In the secular bloc, the class line is particularly important because of the absence of cohesion provided by a common religious outlook. It is, therefore, more accurate to speak of two separate secular blocs: a Liberal bloc, consisting of the secular upper middle and middle classes, and a Socialist bloc consisting of the secular lower middle and lower classes. Thus, unlike ancient Gaul, Holland is divided in four rather than in three parts: Catholics, Calvinists, Socialists, and Liberals.[9]

POLITICAL PARTIES

The fourfold division of Dutch society is manifested in virtually all politically and socially relevant organizations and group affiliations. First of all, each bloc has its own political party. The Roman Catholics have the Catholic People's party which has usually received about 30 per cent of the popular vote in the seven postwar parlia-

[8] The UNESCO survey also found a high degree of class consciousness in the Netherlands as measured by the self-stratification of occupational groups. See Buchanan and Cantril, pp. 14–16. See also F. van Heek and E. V. W. Vercruijsse, "De Nederlandse beroepsprestigestratificatie," in F. van Heek and G. Kuiper, eds., *Sociale stijging en daling in Nederland* (Leyden: H. E. Stenfert Kroese, 1958), pp. 11–48.

[9] This definition of blocs is slightly different from Kruijt's. Kruijt limits the term *zuilen* to those blocs that deliberately seek an isolated and self-contained existence. This restricts its application to the Catholic, Calvinist, and pre–1945 Socialist blocs. See J. P. Kruijt, *Verzuiling* (Zaandijk: Heijnis, 1959), esp. pp. 19–20; Kruijt, "Sociologische beschouwingen over zuilen en verzuiling," *Socialisme en Democratie*, Vol. 14, No. 1 (January 1957), p. 15; and Kruijt, "Verzuildheid in Nederland, blijvende structuur of aflopende episode?" in P. H. van Gorkum, ed., *Pacificatie en de zuilen* (Meppel: J. A. Boom, 1965), pp. 12–16. See also Goudsblom, pp. 30–33, 50–57, 124–126; Moberg, pp. 333–337.

mentary elections. The Socialist bloc has the Labor party with also close to 30 per cent of the vote, and the Liberal bloc the Liberal party (official name: People's Party for Freedom and Democracy) with about 10 per cent of the popular vote. The Calvinist bloc is represented by two parties: the Anti-Revolutionary party (also about 10 per cent) and the Christian Historical Union (slightly below 10 per cent). The original difference between these two Protestant parties was mainly denominational, but also involved a class dimension. The higher class Christian Historicals broke away from the Anti-Revolutionary party of the "little people." Today the main differences are the stronger organization and greater orthodoxy of the Anti-Revolutionaries as compared with the Christian Historicals.

Together, these five parties have usually occupied about 90 per cent of the 150 seats in the Second Chamber, the lower house of the Dutch legislature, since the Second World War. In the 1967 elections, however, the smaller parties managed to reduce this percentage to 82. The small parties in the postwar Second Chambers also fit the basic four-bloc pattern of Dutch society. The Catholic National party, represented in the Chamber from 1948 to 1956, was an ultra-conservative offshoot of the Catholic party. The Pacifist Socialist party and the Communist party are representatives of the fringe of the Socialist bloc. The Political Reformed party and the Reformed Political League are two more Protestant parties representing the most fundamentalist among Dutch Calvinists. The Farmers party, which entered the Chamber for the first time in 1963, and the Democrats '66, established in 1966 and elected to the Chamber in 1967, cannot be assigned as easily to one of the four blocs. Both their leaders and their voters have heterogeneous backgrounds. Ideologically, however, they both belong to the secular bloc: the Democrats '66 on the left and the Farmers party on the extreme right.[10]

[10] See below, pp. 164–167.

The five major parties reflect the present religious and class cleavages. These cleavages were also behind the emergence of the five parties in the late nineteenth century. The principal religious issue was the question of state aid to private denominational schools, and the main class issue was the hotly contested extension of the suffrage. On the education issue, the Liberals who wanted to limit public funds to public (i.e. state) schools were opposed by the Anti-Revolutionaries and the Catholic party who desired public assistance for their own Protestant and Catholic schools. The right to vote caused further splits. The Christian Historicals were conservative on this issue and split away from the Anti-Revolutionary party. Similarly, the left-wing Liberals seceded from the Liberal party and remained in existence as a separate party until the Second World War. After the war they joined with the Socialists and some smaller groups to set up the Labor party.

The relative strengths of the five parties have remained remarkably constant since the first elections under universal manhood suffrage in 1918. Party loyalties have usually been strong and the popular vote very stable; the practically pure proportional representation system has faithfully translated this stable vote into a stable party composition in the First and Second chambers.[11] The most striking illustration of the constancy of Dutch voting behavior is the fate of the Labor party after the Second World War. Before the war its predecessor—the Social Democratic Labor party—directed its appeal almost exclusively at the workers of the secular bloc. The postwar Labor party was a fusion of the prewar

[11] The gross election results tend to exaggerate the degree of stability somewhat, because they mask the changes of those floating voters who neutralize each other's shifting electoral preferences. See H. Daalder, "Politiek in Nederlands kader," in *Mensen en Machten* (Utrecht: Spectrum, 1965), pp. 99–112. See also J. P. A. Gruijters, " 'Wisselende kiezers' bij de verkiezingen van 23 maart 1966: Enige gegevens uit een Amsterdams onderzoek," *Acta Politica*, Vol. 2, No. 1 (1966–67), pp. 3–28.

Social Democrats, left-wing Liberals, and progressive Catholics and Protestants. It sought to break through the barriers separating the secular bloc from the Catholic and Calvinist blocs, and to become a broadly based progressive party. But it failed to make significant inroads into traditional Catholic and Protestant voting strength. In the first postwar elections (1946), the Labor party received fewer votes than the separate parties that had merged into the new party, had received before the war.[12] Subsequent elections did not change the pattern. In the 1956 elections, a peak of 32.7 per cent was reached, up from 28.3 per cent in 1946. But in 1963, it was back to 28 per cent, and the party suffered further losses in 1967.

Evidence of the strong support by the four religious-ideological blocs for their own political parties can be found in the results of various opinion polls. For the purpose of the present study, a national survey was conducted in November 1964.[13] The data on party preference are presented in Tables 3 through 6. Table 3 shows the class composition of the political parties as measured by socioeconomic status ratings assigned by the interviewers. The categories are the usual four, from A (highest) to D (lowest), with an additional rating of high or low within each category. The socioeconomic composition of the Catholic party supporters is

[12] H. Daalder, "Nationale politieke stelsels: Nederland," in L. van der Land, ed., *Repertorium van de sociale wetenschappen: Politiek* (Amsterdam: Elsevier, 1958), p. 230.

[13] The size of the sample was 1282. However, all tables based on the November 1964 survey use a weighted sample of 1,600 which is more representative than the original smaller sample, although the differences are usually slight. The apparent overrepresentation of Labor-party supporters in the weighted sample compared with the other parties may be explained partly by the relatively high number of respondents who did not disclose their party preference (18 per cent). In some tables the total is less than 1,600 due to a small number of nonclassifiable answers or refusals to answer questions like frequency of church attendance. The survey was conducted by the Netherlands Foundation for Statistics in The Hague.

TABLE 3.   SOCIOECONOMIC STATUS AND PARTY PREFERENCE

(In per cent)

Status	Catholic party (333)	Labor party (469)	Liberal party (142)	Anti-Rev. party (143)	Chr. Hist. Union (148)	Other parties (85)	Don't know (280)	Total sample (1,600)
A (high)	4	0	18	1	5	1	4	4
A (low)	3	1	11	6	5	5	4	4
B (high)	14	9	25	18	14	9	10	13
B (low)	23	15	28	28	24	25	23	22
C (high)	30	44	15	30	32	22	32	33
C (low)	19	21	1	8	10	20	17	16
D (high)	6	9	1	5	5	14	7	7
D (low)	1	2	0	3	4	4	3	2

almost exactly the same as that of the sample as a whole. With only minor qualifications, the same applies to the adherents of the two principal Protestant parties. They are more strongly represented by the two highest socioeconomic groups (A and B) than the total sample but the differences are only slight. This is not true for the Labor and Liberal parties. Here class differences appear clearly. The Labor party receives its strongest support from people in the lower classes, especially group C. The Liberal party, on the other hand, is most strongly represented among the high status A and B groups. Socioeconomic status is, of course, only an approximation of social class, rather than its equivalent. But Table 3 still gives a good picture of the class composition of the clienteles of the major parties. The three religious parties are clearly not based on class differences, whereas the two secular parties have a class basis.

Another approximation of social class is occupation. The survey data presented in Table 4 confirm the general picture given by Table 3. Compared with the occupational composition of the total sample, the adherents of the three religious parties are quite evenly distributed among the several occupations. In particular, the clientele of the Catholic party, and to only a slightly lesser extent that of the Christian Historical Union, are almost mirror images of the sample as a whole. The only striking differences are their strong support among farmers. Farmers are also disproportionately represented among the clientele of the Anti-Revolutionary party. This party is weak among blue-collar workers and comparatively strong among businessmen, professionals, and white-collar workers. All of these differences are very slight, however, compared with the occupational differences between the supporters of the two secular parties. The Labor party receives strong support from blue-collar workers and is underrepresented among all other groups. The Liberals receive less of their support from blue-collar workers than any other

TABLE 4. OCCUPATION AND PARTY PREFERENCE

(In per cent)

Occupation	Catholic party (333)	Labor party (465)	Liberal party (142)	Anti-Rev. party (143)	Chr. Hist. Union (147)	Other parties (85)	Don't know (280)	Total sample (1,595)
Businessmen	12	4	24	13	7	14	16	11
Professionals	2	2	5	5	3	4	4	3
White-collar workers	23	21	35	29	29	16	22	24
Blue-collar workers	34	48	11	17	30	42	28	34
Farmers	8	0	1	8	7	7	2	4
Farm workers	2	1	0	1	3	2	0	1
No occupation	19	22	25	27	21	14	28	23

party, and are especially strong among businessmen and white-collar workers.

If class is a major factor for only two of the five big parties, religion affects all parties very much, as Table 5 demonstrates. In this table, Catholics and members of the Dutch Reformed Church are both divided into two groups: the "regulars," who attend church at least once a week, and the "irregulars," who attend church only occasionally or never. Church attendance is only a very crude indicator of religious commitment, but it is important to make some distinction of this kind, although not more than a rough approximation is possible. As stated earlier, religious affiliation alone is not a valid criterion of membership in the subcultural blocs, especially in the case of the Dutch Reformed and Roman Catholic churches. The more committed and more orthodox members belong to the Catholic and Calvinist blocs, whereas the less committed freethinkers belong to the secular bloc. The table also shows the party preferences of each of the three blocs combined. The Catholic bloc coincides with the Catholic regulars. The Calvinist bloc consists of the Dutch Reformed regulars and all members of the Reformed Church. The secular bloc (i.e. the Liberal plus the Socialist blocs) comprises those without religious affiliation, the Dutch Reformed and Catholic irregulars, and the few adherents of other religions—on the not altogether unquestionable assumption that they are "dissenters," and liberal rather than orthodox. These operational criteria for dividing the sample into the three blocs are again only rough approximations but they are essential if survey methods are to be employed. Incidentally, they lead to slight understatements of the strengths of the Catholic and Calvinist blocs (25 and 20 per cent) and an exaggeration of the size of the secular bloc (56 per cent).

Four of the five main parties draw about 90 per cent of their support from a single bloc. The Catholic party gets 90

TABLE 5. RELIGION AND PARTY PREFERENCE
(In per cent)

Religion	Catholic party (328)	Labor party (462)	Liberal party (141)	Anti-Rev. party (143)	Chr. Hist. Union (147)	Other parties (83)	Don't know (266)	Total sample (1,570)
Catholic (regular)	90	6	5	2	1	2	20	25
Catholic (irregular)	9	7	9	0	1	2	11	7
Reformed	0	2	1	71	8	20	6	10
Dutch Reformed (regular)	0	3	4	15	61	4	7	10
Dutch Reformed (irregular)	1	41	39	8	22	16	17	22
Other religions	0	4	4	3	5	8	5	4
No religion	0	37	39	1	2	47	34	23
Catholic bloc	90	6	5	2	1	2	20	25
Secular bloc	10	89	90	12	30	73	67	56
Calvinist bloc	0	5	5	87	69	24	13	20

per cent of its votes from the Catholic bloc alone, only 10 per cent from the secular bloc and virtually no support from the Calvinist bloc. Moreover, 9 of the 10 per cent secular-bloc members are Catholics—the irregulars. The Labor party receives 89 per cent of its votes from the secular bloc, mainly from Dutch Reformed irregulars and persons without religious affiliations. The remainder of its support is about equally divided between the Catholic and Calvinist blocs. The same description fits the Liberal party: 90 per cent of its support is derived from the secular bloc, mainly the ir-religious and the Dutch Reformed irregulars, and the remain-ing 10 per cent in about equal proportions from the other two blocs. Members of the Calvinist bloc constitute the mainstay of the Anti-Revolutionary party: 87 per cent, of which 71 per cent are adherents of the Reformed Church. Its remaining votes are contributed primarily by Dutch Re-formed irregulars.

The picture is less clearcut for the less orthodox Christian Historical Union, even though this party receives no less than two-thirds (69 per cent) of its votes from the Calvinist bloc alone. Its other support is mainly derived from the secular bloc: 30 per cent, of which 22 per cent are Dutch Reformed irregulars.

To get an over-all impression of the pattern of sharp re-ligious and class cleavages underlying party loyalties, the data on socioeconomic status and bloc membership were combined in Table 6. The supporters of each of the five big parties were divided into three blocs: Catholic, secular, and Calvinist; and two classes: middle class (socioeconomic status A and B) and lower class (status groups C and D). The percentage of support which a party received from each of the six cells was then compared with the percentage of the total sample belonging to that cell. The indices of rela-tive party preference indicate the degree to which a party received more or less support from a particular segment of the population than the proportion of that segment among the population as a whole. For instance, let us assume that lower-class Catholics constitute 10 per cent of the population, and also 10 per cent of the supporters of the Labor party. Then the index of party preference of lower-class Catholics for the Labor party is zero per cent: that is, the support of lower-class Catholics for the Labor party is exactly as strong as their proportion of the total sample. If, on the other hand, lower-class Catholics constitute only 7 per cent of the Labor party voters, the index of party preference is −30 per cent: that is, they support the Labor party 30 per cent *less* than what one would have "expected" from the size of the group among the whole sample. A final example: if lower-class Catholics constitute as much as 15 per cent of Labor party voting strength compared with their share of only 10 per cent of the total population, their index of party preference for Labor is +50 per cent: that is, 50 per cent more than what one would have expected.[14]

None of the five major parties can claim to represent a cross-section of the people. In fact, the deviations from the hypothetical pattern of equal distribution are extreme (see Table 6). It is also noteworthy that more than two-thirds of the indices are negative and less than a third positive. This means that the parties are the virtually exclusive representatives of relatively small class and religious segments of the population and receive very little backing from any other segments. The Catholic party receives two to three times

[14] The exact formula used to calculate the index of relative party preference is as follows: if *N* stands for the size of the total sample, *A* for the size of the cell in the total sample, *n* for the total number of party supporters, and *a* the number of party supporters in the particular cell, the index is:

$$\frac{a - n\dfrac{A}{N}}{n\dfrac{A}{N}} \times 100\% \text{ or } \left(\frac{aN}{An} - 1\right) \times 100\%$$

more support from Catholics of all classes than what one
would have expected from the proportion of Catholics
among the total population. Conversely, the secular bloc
supports this party about 80 per cent less than expected, and

TABLE 6.   INDICES OF RELATIVE PARTY PREFERENCE

Party		Catholic	Secular	Calvinist
Catholic (N-328)	Middle	+274	−79	−97
	Lower	+254	−84	−100
Labor (N-462)	Middle	−94	−1	−82
	Lower	−61	+101	−72
Liberal (N-141)	Middle	−52	+239	−77
	Lower	−100	−55	−72
Anti-Rev. (N-143)	Middle	−93	−72	+389
	Lower	−90	−83	+291
Chr. Hist.	Middle	−93	−36	+260
Union (N-147)	Lower	−95	−53	+240

the Calvinists contribute practically nothing at all—an index of −100 per cent means that the number of cases in that
cell was zero. The Labor party receives outstanding support
from lower-class members of the secular bloc, only indiffer-
ent support from middle-class seculars, and a striking lack
of support from all other groups. The Liberal party also gets
most of its strength from the secular bloc, but only from
the middle class. Of the two Protestant parties, the Anti-
Revolutionaries get three to four times more support from
the Calvinist bloc than expected and virtually no backing at
all from the secular and Catholic blocs. The dividing line
between Calvinists and seculars is somewhat less sharp for
the Christian Historical Union: the negative indices of party
preference of the secular bloc are less extreme than most of
the negative indices. Otherwise, the pattern is very similar
to the Anti-Revolutionary party.

The neat coincidence of blocs and parties would probably

be closer still if we could refine our criteria for assigning respondents to a particular bloc. In fact, an alternative operational criterion for bloc membership would be party preference itself. A supporter of the Catholic party would then *ipso facto* be regarded as belonging to the Catholic bloc. Supporters of the two Protestant parties would be assigned to the Calvinist bloc. The Labor party clientele would be regarded as the Socialist bloc and the Liberal clientele as the Liberal bloc. The only drawbacks of using this criterion are that some voters—although not many—cast their votes not according to bloc loyalty but on the basis of special issues or personalities. A practical disadvantage is that it limits the usable size of the sample to those respondents who indicated a preference for one of the major five parties (77 per cent), excluding the minor party supporters and the many respondents who did not know or refused to disclose their party preference. In subsequent tables and analyses, party preference will be used as indicators of bloc membership along with religion, church attendance, and socio-economic status.

Traditional loyalties and personal inclination are the most important motives for the nearly solid support by the members of each of the blocs for their own party. But for the Catholic and Calvinist blocs there is also a great deal of admonition from the church. Members of the Reformed—but not the Dutch Reformed—Church are told to support the Anti-Revolutionary party, and Catholics are admonished to support the Catholic party. In his parliamentary history of the interwar years, P. J. Oud recalls the agitation by the Roman Catholic bishops against both the Socialists and a small dissident Catholic party in the national elections of 1922.[15] The most recent *cause célèbre* was the 1954 pastoral letter by the Catholic bishops which was directed mainly against the Labor party. Neither membership in other parties (except the Communist party) nor voting for them

[15] P. J. Oud, *Het jongste verleden: Parlementaire geschiedenis van Nederland 1918–1940*, 6 vols. (Assen: Van Gorcum, 1948–51), Vol. 2, p. 41.

was specifically prohibited, but the letter emphasized the necessity of preserving Roman Catholic unity and condemned liberalism, socialism, and communism. It further urged "that all Catholics become members of the social organizations set up for them" even if their membership could only be a passive one, and forbade—on no less of a penalty than exclusion from the holy sacraments—membership of the Socialist labor union, regular attendance at Socialist meetings, and regular attention to Socialist newspapers and radio broadcasts.[16] The message could hardly have been clearer. It is no coincidence, of course, that the highest percentages of party support in Table 5 are Catholic support of the Catholic party and Reformed support of the Anti-Revolutionaries.

INTEREST GROUPS

The Dutch labor-union movement also reflects the basic four-bloc pattern. About 40 per cent of Dutch workers are union members. The large majority of the unions belong to one of the three main labor-union federations. The largest is the Socialist labor union (N.V.V.) with a membership of 35.7 per cent of all labor-union members in Holland in January 1963. The second largest union is the Catholic labor union (N.K.V.) with a membership of 29.2 per cent. The third is the Protestant labor union (C.N.V.) with 15.8 per cent of organized labor. In addition to these three large Socialist, Catholic, and Protestant unions, there is the small Netherlands Trade Association (N.V.C.) which is ideologically oriented toward the Liberals. It is strong only among higher civil servants and white-collar workers, and its membership includes no more than 0.7 per cent of all organized workers.[17]

[16] Bisschoppelijk mandement, *De Katholiek in het openbare leven van deze tijd* (Utrecht: 1954), esp. pp. 11–14, 22, 35–45.

[17] Centraal Bureau voor de Statistiek, *Omvang der vakbeweging in Nederland op 1 januari 1963* (Zeist: De Haan, 1963), p. 8. See also Daalder, in *Repertorium*, pp. 231–232.

Union membership, as expected, is closely related to membership in the religious-ideological blocs. Tables 7 and 8 present the results of the November 1964 survey on this point. The relevant question inquired into either the respondent's own union membership or that of the respondent's

TABLE 7. RELIGION AND LABOR-UNION MEMBERSHIP

(In per cent)

Religion	Socialist union (209)	Catholic union (108)	Protestant union (109)	Other unions (162)	Total sample (1,570)
Catholic (regular)	1	94	2	31	25
Catholic (irregular)	4	5	1	6	7
Reformed	2	0	41	13	10
Dutch Reformed (regular)	5	0	36	6	10
Dutch Reformed (irregular)	36	0	17	17	22
Other religions	7	0	3	2	4
No religion	44	2	0	24	23
Catholic bloc	1	94	2	31	25
Secular bloc	92	6	21	50	56
Calvinist bloc	7	0	77	19	20

spouse. The Socialist union derives 92 per cent of its strength from the secular bloc and most of the remainder from Dutch Reformed regulars. The Catholic union gets no less than 94 per cent of its members from the Catholic bloc and an additional 5 per cent from Catholics who do not attend church regularly. Membership of the Protestant labor union appears to be the least closely related to bloc membership, although this union still gets as much as 77 per cent of its members from this bloc alone; and another 17 per cent is derived from Dutch Reformed irregulars.

Union membership is even more closely related to party
preference (Table 8). Members of the Socialist labor union

TABLE 8.   PARTY PREFERENCE AND LABOR-UNION MEMBERSHIP
(In per cent)

Party	Socialist union (211)	Catholic union (110)	Protestant union (111)	Other unions (165)	Total sample (1,600)
Catholic	1	81	0	27	21
Labor	78	8	14	23	29
Liberal	1	1	0	12	9
Anti-Revolutionary	2	0	33	10	9
Chr. Hist. Union	2	0	35	7	9
Other	5	1	8	10	5
Don't know	11	9	9	11	18

support the Labor party in overwhelming numbers and give
only negligible support to the other four big parties. Similarly, Catholic union members give almost exclusive support to the Catholic party, and Protestant union members
back the Anti-Revolutionary party and Christian Historical
Union. The only major exception is the moderate backing
for the Labor party among both Catholic and Protestant
labor-union members. This does not change the over-all picture, however: bloc loyalty is the most prominent factor behind union affiliation, too.

As in the case of party preference, the selection of a trade
union is not an entirely free choice that the Dutch worker
can make without church interference. The principal threat
to bloc cohesion among Catholics and Calvinists is the Socialist labor union. The Synod of the Reformed Church declared in 1920 "that a member of the Reformed Church
must not belong to an organization based on the principle
of class struggle [i.e. the Socialist union]." This prohibition

was specifically reaffirmed by synodical edicts in the early 1950's.[18] The Anti-Revolutionary party took a similar stand. In 1953, the party's monthly journal discussed the question of whether a Socialist union member could also become a member of the Anti-Revolutionary party. The answer was that all Anti-Revolutionaries should belong to the Calvinist social organizations, and that if a Socialist union member applying for membership in a local branch of the party "cannot be convinced that this [belonging to the Socialist labor union] is wrong, he should not be admitted."[19] The 1954 pastoral letter by the Roman Catholic bishops argued against membership by Catholics in non-Catholic unions and specifically prohibited affiliation with the Socialist union—a prohibition enforced by denial of the holy sacraments.[20] Few members of the Catholic and Reformed Churches ignore these dictates, as Table 7 demonstrates.

Intervention by the Catholic bishops was also responsible for blocking the growth of a joint Catholic-Protestant labor-union movement in the early decades of the twentieth century. Around 1900 there were a number of interdenominational Christian farmers organizations and labor unions, but in 1906 the Catholic bishops rejected the idea of Catholic-Protestant cooperation within a single organization.[21] The decisive turning point came in 1912 with the episcopal prohibition of membership in the interdenominational textile-workers union—appropriately named Unitas—in the East-

[18] C. J. Verplanke, "De Gereformeerde gezindte en de christelijke organisatie," *Anti-Revolutionaire Staatkunde*, Vol. 33, No. 11 (November 1963), pp. 332–335.

[19] *Anti-Revolutionaire Staatkunde*, Vol. 23, No. 3 (March 1953), pp. 124–125, quoted in a letter by P. F. van Herwijnen of the Doctor Abraham Kuyperstichting (dated November 11, 1966) to the author. See also below, pp. 197–198.

[20] *Bisschoppelijk mandement*, pp. 27–30, 42–43. But see also below, p. 198.

[21] Kruijt and Goddijn, p. 236. W. Banning, *Hedendaagse sociale bewegingen: Achtergronden en beginselen* (7th ed., Arnhem: Van Loghum, Slaterus, 1962), pp. 75–76.

ern textile-industry region of the Netherlands. Unitas was a strong and successful union in which cooperation between Catholics and Protestants thrived. The conditions for cooperation were extremely favorable; frictions between the churches had long been minimal in the area; the idea of interfaith cooperation was stimulated from across the border by the Cologne school in the German Catholic labor-union movement; and cooperation with the Protestants offered Catholic workers better opportunities for bargaining with their employers, most of whom were Dutch Reformed. In 1912, a decree by the archbishop was read in the Catholic churches in the region enjoining all Catholics from further participation in Unitas. Virtually all Catholic workers obeyed and left the union, though it took four years of intensive efforts by the clergy before they started to join the new separate Catholic union in sizable numbers.[22]

The bloc pattern of Dutch society reflected in the labor-union movements also characterizes the employers, farmers, farm workers, and retailers organizations. There are three employers associations: Catholic, Protestant, and Liberal; three farmers organizations: again, Catholic, Protestant, and Liberal; three farm workers unions: a Catholic one, affiliated with the large Catholic labor union N.K.V., a Protestant one affiliated with the Protestant C.N.V., and a Socialist one affiliated with the Socialist N.V.V. Finally, retailers associations are also split into separate Catholic, Protestant, and Liberal organizations.

MEDIA OF COMMUNICATION

Each bloc has its own newspapers, too, though not to the exclusion of a number of truly independent nonbloc papers. The size of each bloc press in recent years is presented in Table 9. A comparison of the circulation fig-

[22] F. van Heek, *Het geboorte-niveau der Nederlandse Rooms-Katholieken* (Leyden: H. E. Stenfert Kroese, 1954), pp. 165–167.

TABLE 9. STRENGTHS OF BLOC AND NONBLOC NEWSPAPERS
(In per cent)

Newspapers	Circulation		
	1955	1964	1966
Catholic	26.4	26.8	27.0
Socialist	19.3	16.1	14.4
Protestant	8.7	8.2	6.6
Liberal	5.1	4.6	4.3
Neutral	40.5	44.3	47.7

NOTE: The Communist press is excluded from the table.
SOURCE: Data supplied by M. Rooij of the University of Amsterdam in a letter (dated February 15, 1967) to the author.

ures of all daily papers (except the small Communist press, omitted from the table) with the strengths of the principal parties shows that the Catholic press is the most strongly developed—undoubtedly aided by the 1954 episcopal edict to all Catholics "to support these [Catholic newspapers] and these alone."[23] The Protestant press is the weakest, and the Socialist and Liberal papers are in an intermediate position. It should be noted that an increasing percentage of the total newspaper circulation—almost half in 1966— is produced by independent papers. The nonbloc press is especially strong among local and regional papers.

The relative weakness of the Protestant press is apparent at the national level, too. Among the dozen or so "national" newspapers—which are read throughout the country and which are the principal opinion makers—there is only one Protestant paper: the Anti-Revolutionary *Trouw*. The Christian Historical Union has no national daily at all. The two independent (but right-wing) national dailies constitute the Dutch yellow press: *De Telegraaf* and *De Courant Nieuws van de Dag*. The other national newspapers fit the bloc pattern closely: *De Volkskrant* and *De Tijd* are Catholic, *Het*

[23] Bisschoppelijk mandement, p. 36.

TABLE 10. RELIGION AND THE PRESS

(In per cent)

Religion	Newspapers						
	Catholic	Protestant	Socialist	Liberal	Independent	None	Total
Catholic (regular)	87	0	3	1	12	4	107
Catholic (irregular)	38	1	22	2	42	6	111
Reformed	2	66	4	3	33	7	115
Dutch Reformed (regular)	2	20	18	7	58	7	112
Dutch Reformed (irregular)	2	4	33	7	65	5	116
Other religions	3	9	32	15	65	3	127
No religion	2	2	48	10	55	3	120
Total sample	30	10	22	6	42	5	115

NOTES: The term "regular" in this table refers to those respondents who attended church at least once in the three weeks prior to the interview.—The percentages add up to more than 100 because of multiple responses.—Communist papers are omitted from the table.

SOURCE: Adapted from Centraal Bureau voor de Statistiek, *Vrije-tijdsbesteding in Nederland Winter 1955/'56: Deel 4, Leesgewoonten* (Zeist: De Haan, 1957), p. 62.

Vrije Volk and *Het Parool* are Socialist, and four national dailies are Liberal: *Algemeen Handelsblad, Algemeen Dagblad, Nieuwe Rotterdamse Courant,* and *Het Vaderland.*

Table 10 presents the results of a sample survey conducted in 1955 and 1956 by the Central Bureau of Statistics. The respondents were asked which newspaper or newspapers they read, and these were then classified according to the readers' religious or ideological orientation. Particularly Catholic regulars and Reformed persons show overwhelming preference for their own newspapers. Among all other groups, independent papers enjoy considerable popularity, but reading of a newspaper of another bloc is rare. Few secular-bloc members (the irreligious, Dutch Reformed irregulars, and so on) read Catholic or Protestant papers; few of the Catholic bloc read Protestant, Socialist, or Liberal papers; and few members of the Calvinist bloc read Catholic, Socialist, or Liberal papers. The only major exception is the high degree of attention by Dutch Reformed regulars to the Socialist and Liberal press (18 and 7 per cent) compared with their attention to the Protestant press (20 per cent). This deviation from bloc conformity may possibly be the result of the rather lenient definition of regular church attendance used in the survey (see note 1 in Table 10). The same 1955–1956 survey also found that most persons receive their news and editorial comments from only one ideological source: 87 per cent. Only 9 per cent read papers belonging to different blocs.[24]

The national newspapers circulate even more exclusively among their own blocs. Tables 11 and 12 show the results of the November 1964 survey. No less than 90 per cent of the readers of the two Catholic national dailies belong to the Catholic bloc, and another 6 per cent are Catholic irregulars. Similarly, 90 per cent of the readers of the Anti-Revolution-

[24] Centraal Bureau voor de Statistiek, *Vrije-tijdsbesteding: Leesgewoonten,* pp. 64–65.

TABLE 11. RELIGION AND THE NATIONAL NEWSPAPERS
(In per cent)

Religion	Newspapers					
	Catholic (86)	Calvinist (60)	Socialist (223)	Liberal (123)	Independent (187)	Total (1,570)
Catholic (regular)	90	3	1	6	13	25
Catholic (irregular)	6	2	5	7	10	7
Reformed	1	63	4	6	6	10
Dutch Reformed (regular)	0	27	1	12	9	10
Dutch Reformed (irregular)	3	5	33	27	26	22
Other religions	0	0	5	11	7	4
No religion	0	0	51	31	29	23
Catholic bloc	90	3	1	6	13	25
Secular bloc	9	7	94	76	72	56
Calvinist bloc	1	90	5	19	15	20

ary paper *Trouw* belong to the Calvinist bloc, and another 5 per cent to Dutch Reformed irregulars. The secular bloc accounts for 94 per cent of the readers of the two Socialist dailies. The figures for the Liberal press are less striking: a relatively low 74 per cent of their readers belong to the secular bloc, and a relatively high 19 per cent to the Calvinist bloc (compared with their 20 per cent share of the total sample). The independent papers are more equally distributed, but their main strength lies with the secular bloc. Because Catholics and Calvinists strongly prefer their own newspapers, the independent papers become to some extent secular-bloc papers by default. Table 12 confirms the overall picture. The Catholic, Calvinist, and Socialist newspapers are read almost exclusively by supporters of the Catholic, Anti-Revolutionary, and Labor parties. The Liberal press has a wider popularity although its most significant strength is among Liberal party adherents. Supporters of the Christian Historical Union who do not have their own national newspaper are most strongly represented among the readers of the Calvinist *Trouw* and the Liberal press.

In the discussion of the clienteles of the national newspapers so far, the two Catholic, the two Socialist, the four Liberal, and the two independent papers were combined. This hides one interesting phenomenon: a pronounced class difference within each of these groups. The clientele of the Catholic *De Volkskrant* is more middle than lower class: 62 per cent belong to socioeconomic groups A and B and 38 per cent to groups C and D. But the clientele of *De Tijd* is much more strongly middle class: its class distribution is 96–4 compared with 62–38 for *De Volkskrant*. Of the independent papers, the comparable figure for *De Telegraaf* is 69–31, compared with 23–77 for *De Courant Nieuws van de Dag*. These differences appear even among the already class-based Socialist and Liberal papers. For the Socialist *Het Vrije Volk* and *Het Parool* the figures are 24–76 and 44–56. And for the Liberal *Algemeen Dagblad* they are 64–36, compared

TABLE 12. PARTY PREFERENCE AND THE NATIONAL NEWSPAPERS
(In per cent)

| Party | Newspapers | | | | | |
	Catholic (89)	Calvinist (60)	Socialist (223)	Liberal (125)	Independent (195)	Total (1,600)
Catholic	72	0	2	6	12	21
Labor	4	0	68	21	24	29
Liberal	6	0	6	32	22	9
Anti-Revolutionary	1	77	2	8	5	9
Chr. Hist. Union	1	18	3	14	11	9
Other	1	2	7	6	5	5
Don't know	15	3	12	13	21	18

with a lopsided 97–3 for the other three Liberal dailies combined.[25]

It is significant that the bloc pattern of the Dutch press persisted even in the underground press during the five years of German occupation in the Second World War. Of the five principal clandestine publications, four had definite bloc connections. *Vrij Nederland* was originally founded by young Calvinists but later became exclusively secular and pro-Socialist. *Het Parool* was also Socialist, *Trouw* was Calvinist, and *De Waarheid* was Communist. Only one of the illegal publications transcended bloc lines: *Je Maintiendrai*. It included a diverse group of Catholics, Protestants, and secular people.[26] It is perhaps even more significant that the four bloc-oriented papers continued in existence as dailies or weeklies after the Second World War, whereas the more broadly based *Je Maintiendrai* did not survive the end of war and occupation.

The other media of communication—radio and television —fall into the four-bloc pattern even more clearly than the press. Radio and television in the Netherlands are state-owned but not state-operated. Programming is in the hands of private organizations with large dues-paying memberships. Each of the organizations is entitled to a share of broadcasting and telecasting time roughly proportional to the size of its membership. Four of these associations, which are approximately equal in size, represent the four blocs: K.R.O. (Catholic), N.C.R.V. (Calvinist), V.A.R.A. (Socialist), and A.V.R.O. (Liberal, though it prefers to call itself a "general" organization and formally avoids the label "Liberal").

[25] These percentages are all based on rather small totals. But they are, on the whole, confirmed by a survey held in the early 1960's which used a very large sample: N=47,159. See Nederlands Instituut voor de Publieke Opinie, *Nationaal Advertentiemedia Onderzoek* (Amsterdam, ca. 1962), Table 48.

[26] Werner Warmbrunn, *The Dutch under German Occupation: 1940–1945* (Stanford: Stanford University Press, 1963), pp. 225–235.

A fifth one (V.P.R.O.) is a liberal Protestant broadcasting association; it is very small and constantly has to struggle for survival.

Membership in the radio and television organizations is closely related to membership in the subcultural blocs (Table 13). The overwhelming majority of the members of the Catholic organization belong to the Catholic bloc (89 per cent); the rest are mainly Catholic irregulars. The Calvinist radio gets 75 per cent of its members from the Calvinist bloc, but also a relatively large 24 per cent from the secular bloc; most of the latter group are Dutch Reformed irregulars. The Socialist radio is almost exclusively supported by people belonging to the secular bloc: 96 per cent. Support for the Liberal radio is also derived mainly from the secular bloc: 86 per cent. The small liberal Protestant organization fits somewhere in between the secular and Calvinist blocs but leans toward the former as far as its membership is concerned.[27] Table 14 shows a similar relationship between membership in the radio and television organizations and party preference. The Catholic radio is supported mainly by adherents of the Catholic Party, the Calvinist radio by Anti-Revolutionaries and Christian Historicals, and the Socialist radio by Socialists. Support for the Liberal and liberal Protestant organizations has a somewhat broader base. The Liberal party supporters back the Liberal radio in significantly large numbers, but the Liberal radio is also supported by many Socialists. The liberal Protestant radio is strong among both Liberals and to a lesser extent among Christian Historicals. Here again, considerable backing comes from Labor-party supporters, too.

[27] See also Nederlands Instituut voor de Publieke Opinie, *Nationaal Advertentiemedia Onderzoek*, Tables 40 and 49; Centraal Bureau voor de Statistiek, *Radio, televisie en vrije-tijdsbesteding herfst 1960* (Zeist: De Haan, 1962), p. 83; and A. Oostindie, "Pacificatie in de omroep," in Van Gorkum, ed., *Pacificatie en de zuilen*, pp. 139–170.

TABLE 13. RELIGION AND MEMBERSHIP IN RADIO-TELEVISION ASSOCIATIONS

(In per cent)

Religion	Radio-Television Associations					
	Catholic (250)	Calvinist (224)	Socialist (207)	Liberal (185)	Liberal-Protestant (63)	Total (1,570)
Catholic (regular)	89	0	1	5	2	25
Catholic (irregular)	8	0	7	10	5	7
Reformed	0	40	0	4	10	10
Dutch Reformed (regular)	0	36	2	4	11	10
Dutch Reformed (irregular)	2	20	35	31	41	22
Other religions	0	3	2	5	8	4
No religion	1	1	52	41	24	23
Catholic bloc	89	0	1	5	2	25
Secular bloc	10	24	96	86	78	56
Calvinist bloc	0	75	3	8	21	20

TABLE 14. PARTY PREFERENCE AND MEMBERSHIP IN RADIO-TELEVISION ASSOCIATIONS

(In per cent)

Party	Radio-Television Associations					
	Catholic (252)	Calvinist (227)	Socialist (209)	Liberal (190)	Liberal-Protestant (63)	Total (1,600)
Catholic	76	0	1	4	0	21
Labor	8	11	76	26	30	29
Liberal	2	1	1	24	29	9
Anti-Revolutionary	0	41	0	2	6	9
Chr. Hist. Union	0	31	2	5	13	9
Other	1	7	4	11	10	5
Don't know	13	9	15	28	13	18

Affiliations with political parties, labor unions, radio associations, and so on, are the most important and politically the most relevant affiliations. The bloc pattern analyzed above characterizes not only these politically significant organizations but also the whole gamut of other voluntary associations: cultural, recreational, sports, youth, and charitable organizations. The 1955–56 survey by the Central Bureau of Statistics inquired into all voluntary associations to which the respondents belonged, and classified each membership according to the religious connection of the organization. Table 15 presents the results. The classification is rather crude: organizational memberships are only divided

TABLE 15.   RELIGION AND MEMBERSHIP IN
VOLUNTARY ASSOCIATIONS
(In per cent)

	Associations			
Religion	Catholic	Dutch Reformed	Other Religious	General
Catholic	77	0	3	20
Reformed	0	6	74	19
Dutch Reformed	1	30	13	56
Other religions	0	3	37	60
No religion	1	2	11	86
Total sample	27	12	17	45

SOURCE: Adapted from Centraal Bureau voor de Statistiek, *Vrijetrijdsbesteding in Nederland Winter 1955/'56: Deel 5, Verenigingsleven* (Zeist: De Haan, 1957), pp. 25–26.

into Catholic, Dutch Reformed, other religious connections, and general; and church attendance by the respondents is not taken into consideration. But the table still presents a useful bird's eye view. The majority of all memberships in voluntary organizations (55 per cent) are in organizations with a religious connection, almost half of which (27 per cent) are Catholic. The strongest loyalties are those of Catholics to Catholic organizations (77 per cent) and of Reformed people to "other"—presumably Reformed—organizations (74 per cent). The general, not religion-based associations have members from all segments but are weakest among Reformed and Catholics and strongest among those without religious affiliations.

EDUCATION AND INTERPERSONAL RELATIONS

By now this tale of four blocs is becoming monotonous. With few exceptions, the religious and class cleavages are apparent in all aspects of organized life. Nowhere is this more true than in education. About a century ago, more than three-fourths of all elementary-school pupils attended public nondenominational schools. The present situation is almost completely reversed. In 1957 only 28 per cent still attended public schools and 72 per cent were in private schools: 43 per cent in Catholic, 27 per cent in Protestant, and 2 per cent in other private schools.[28] This threefold division is not limited to primary schools: a person can be educated from kindergarten to Ph.D. in a school of his religious persuasion. At the university level, public schools still predominate. Of the twelve universities and other institutes of higher learning nine are public. The three private schools are the Calvinist Free University of Amsterdam, the Catholic University in Nijmegen, and the Catholic Institute of Economics in Tilburg. But even at the public universities, extracurricular life is far from integrated: most student clubs are separately organized on a bloc basis.

Education is obviously of vital importance in perpetuating the bloc pattern in Dutch life. Particularly the thorough division of elementary education not only separates the chil-

[28] S. Miedema, "De kosten van de verzuiling," *Socialisme en Democratie*, Vol. 14, No. 1 (January 1957), p. 49; Centraal Bureau voor de Statistiek, *Zestig jaren statistiek in tijdreeksen* (Zeist: De Haan, 1959), p. 31.

dren belonging to different blocs physically but also instills
different values in them. This goes beyond the teaching of
different religious beliefs: the standards emphasized in elementary schools are those of the separate subculture of the
bloc rather than an integrated national culture. National
history as taught in elementary schools is merely the country's past interpreted from each bloc's point of view rather
than a truly national history that is felt as a commonly appre-
ciated and unifying background. I. Gadourek, in his famous
community study of the small western town of Sassenheim,
gives some striking examples. With regard to the crucial
period of the Dutch war of independence, especially the
Catholic and Calvinist versions are far apart. The Inquisition
which did much to foster anti-Spanish and anti-Catholic
sentiments in the Netherlands, is described in the Catholic
history text as "a tribunal of the Church" composed of "wise
and pious bishops and priests," whereas the Calvinist text-
book emphasizes that "each day . . . innocent people were
tortured and murdered. The inquisition was merciless." And
the Catholic verdict on William of Orange, Holland's foremost national hero, is rather equivocal: "We must esteem
Orange as the Founder of our independence but we cannot
by far approve of all his deeds."[29] Gadourek also recounts
that national history is an extremely small part of the elementary school curriculum, and that in teaching Dutch
language grammar is emphasized rather than "the stimula-
tion of a consciousness of national cultural inheritance and
unity."[30]

From kindergarten on, children are separated according
to the bloc to which they belong, unless they live in a community where their bloc is so weakly represented that they
have no special school. Friendships naturally develop within

[29] I. Gadourek, *A Dutch Community: Social and Cultural Structure and Process in a Bulb-Growing Region in the Netherlands* (2nd
ed., Groningen: Wolters, 1961), pp. 545–546.
[30] *Ibid.*, p. 209.

each bloc rather than across different blocs. Is this preval-
ence of intrabloc friendships carried into adulthood? The
November 1964 survey attempted to find an answer to the
question of how strong bloc boundaries are on a personal
level. The respondents were asked: "Now I'd like to ask a
question about your friends, let's say your five best friends.
Here is a list with different groups on it. To which of these
groups do your best friends belong? Any other?" The groups
listed were readily identifiable religious and political groups
like Catholics, people without religion, Socialists, and so on.
These groups approximate, but do not coincide with the subcultural blocs; in particular, the crucial distinction between
the more and the less deeply committed among Dutch Reformed and Catholics could not be made in a question of this
kind.

Tables 16 and 17 show that bloc boundaries are clearly
discernible in interpersonal relationships, but that they are
not "iron curtains" and are sometimes transcended. Of the
total sample, 92 per cent answered the question; many of
them mentioned more than one group to which their best
friends belonged. On the average, one out of every three
respondents had friends belonging to more than one of the
four mutually exclusive religious groups. Intrabloc friendships predominate: 85 per cent of the members of the Catholic bloc had other Catholics among their friends, and much
smaller percentages mentioned other groups; Calvinists had
friends primarily among other Protestants (59 and 61 per
cent); secular-bloc members mentioned mainly the Dutch
Reformed (41 per cent) and people without religion (36 per
cent), but a relatively high 26 per cent indicated that they
had friends among Roman Catholics. When friendship is
crosstabulated with party preference, a similar picture
emerges (see Table 17). Supporters of the Catholic party
show a strong preference for Roman Catholic friends; Labor
party and Liberal party supporters for Dutch Reformed and
irreligious friends—and Labor party supporters for Social-

TABLE 16.   RELIGION AND FRIENDSHIP
(In per cent)

Religion	(Number)	Friends are:								Total
		Catholic	Reformed	Dutch Reformed	Without religion	Socialist	Liberal	Don't know		
Catholics (regular)	(389)	85	9	14	13	3	6	6		136
Catholics (irregular)	(105)	53	7	15	21	14	8	10		128
Reformed	(157)	17	78	38	15	8	10	7		173
Dutch Reformed (regular)	(151)	14	38	85	17	6	9	2		172
Dutch Reformed (irregular)	(351)	23	12	63	23	28	11	8		167
Other religions	(56)	41	25	39	41	18	16	9		189
No religion	(361)	19	12	27	53	26	11	7		156
Catholic bloc	(389)	85	9	14	13	3	6	6		136
Secular bloc	(873)	26	12	41	36	25	11	8		159
Calvinist bloc	(308)	16	59	61	16	7	9	5		172
Total sample	(1570)	39	20	38	26	16	9	8		156

NOTE: Percentages of more than 100 are due to multiple responses.

TABLE 17. PARTY PREFERENCE AND FRIENDSHIP
(In per cent)

| | | | | Friends are: | | | | |
Party	(Number)	Catholic	Reformed	Dutch Reformed	Without religion	Socialist	Liberal	Don't know	Total
Catholic	(333)	86	9	15	12	2	4	8	136
Labor	(469)	27	12	43	34	35	5	4	160
Liberal	(142)	29	13	45	39	6	44	5	181
Anti-Revolutionary	(143)	16	78	48	19	9	8	7	185
Chr. Hist. Union	(148)	19	34	84	15	7	5	3	167
Other	(85)	25	28	33	35	14	12	6	153
Don't know	(280)	34	12	27	30	12	7	15	137
Total sample	(1600)	39	20	38	26	16	9	8	156

NOTE: Percentages of more than 100 are due to multiple responses.

ists, Liberals for other Liberals; Anti-Revolutionaries first for Reformed and second for Dutch Reformed friends, and members of the Christian Historical Union the other way around.

Different and probably more sensitive indicators of the strength of bloc lines in interpersonal relations are attitudes toward interbloc marriage and the incidence of interbloc vis-à-vis intrabloc marriage. The evidence parallels that presented above. According to the 1960 census, 94.7 per cent of all married Catholics had Catholic spouses, and the percentages for the other major groups are only slightly lower: 89.8 per cent for the Dutch Reformed, 93.6 per cent for Reformed people, and 87.1 per cent for persons without religious affiliations.[31] To measure the social distance between denominational groups, Gadourek asked the following question of a sample (N=404) of people in the town of Sassenheim: "Do you approve of your children or brothers and sisters marrying a person of a different religious persuasion? become close friends? work together with such a person?" Interdenominational marriage was rejected by 81.9 per cent of the respondents, friendship by less than half (40.6 per cent) and work by 11.4 per cent.[32]

In practice, the patterns of hiring and patronage are not so free from prejudice and discrimination. Though it is hard to obtain systematic evidence, observers of Dutch society agree that considerable preference is shown by buyers for stores owned by fellow members of their bloc and by employers for job applicants of the same bloc, especially in smaller communities and in small-scale businesses. As J. P. Kruijt points out, this discrimination is often unintentional and even unconscious; it may be merely the symptom of living, moving, and communicating in the strictly bounded world of one's own subculture. But even here intrabloc pref-

[31] G. Dekker, *Het kerkelijk gemengde huwelijk in Nederland* (Meppel: J. A. Boom, n.d.), p. 99.
[32] Gadourek, pp. 112–113.

erence is sometimes officially prescribed. For instance, the Roman Catholic bishops in 1958 issued an instruction to all Catholic institutions that were accountable to them: for all construction projects, only Catholic architects, only contractors organized in Catholic associations, and as much as possible only workers belonging to Catholic labor unions were to be employed. The bishops added: "We confidently expect all governing bodies of Catholic institutions that are not accountable to us to adhere to our stipulations, too."[33]

Thus the blocs live side by side as distinctly separate subcultural communities, each with its own political and social institutions and with interaction and communication across bloc boundaries kept to a minimum. Is this one nation or, to paraphrase Disraeli, several nations inhabiting the same country?

[33] Kruijt, *Verzuiling,* pp. 41–42.

Chapter III

THE FOUR ELITES

INTERLOCKING DIRECTORATES

The four blocs of Dutch society all have their own political and social organizations and also their own leaders. Each of the four elites is a closely knit self-contained group. This strong cohesion is partly the result of formal connections between the political parties, interest groups, and newspapers within each bloc, but an even more important factor is the pattern of informal intrabloc connections formed by the interlocking directorates of the various bloc organizations.

Formal organizational ties occur in a number of cases. The Socialist daily *Het Vrije Volk*—the largest newspaper in the Netherlands—is the official party organ of the Labor party, and is owned jointly by the party and the Socialist labor union. Its editor-in-chief is nominated by the party executive committee and appointed by the party congress.[1]

---

[1] M. Rooij, "Is de Nederlandse pers verzuild?" in P. H. van Gor-

Before the Second World War, the Socialist labor union
(N.V.V.) and the Social Democratic party had formal organizational ties, but these were not continued by the Labor
party after the war. The Roman Catholic daily *De Volkskrant* is formally linked with the Catholic labor union. Another major Catholic newspaper, *De Maasbode*, always had
at least one priest on its editorial board, and was required
by its bylaws to follow the advice of the bishop of Haarlem
if the directors and editors were in disagreement on specifically religious questions or Catholic interests. This newspaper merged with the Catholic *De Tijd* several years ago,
and the joint *De Tijd-De Maasbode* is, like *De Tijd* before
the merger, a Roman Catholic paper but controlled by laymen and without formal connections with the church. The
name *De Maasbode* has now been dropped completely except in the Rotterdam edition of the paper.[2] Only the various
Communist organizations formally maintain complete organizational unity. The elites of the four subcultural blocs
rely mainly on informal connections.

Intrabloc overlapping memberships in the governing
bodies of the bloc institutions are clear symptoms of the co-
hesiveness of each of the four elites. The situation in the
early 1960's will be analyzed in order to get an insight into
this pattern.[3] The listing will not be exhaustive. Only ties
between the major bloc institutions will be examined: party
organizations, the parties' parliamentary delegations, labor
unions, employers, retailers, and farmers associations, farm
workers unions, radio and television organizations, news-

---

kum, ed., *Pacificatie en de zuilen* (Meppel: J. A. Boom, 1965), pp.
78–79.

[2] Letter by M. Rooij of the University of Amsterdam (dated October 28, 1966) to the author.

[3] The data on which the following analysis is based can be found
in two annual publications: *Parlement en Kiezer* (The Hague: Nijhoff), and *Pyttersen's Nederlandse Almanak* (Zaltbommel: Van de
Garde).

papers, and the twelve universities and other institutions of higher learning. If during the three or four years of the early 1960's several leaders occupied the same or a comparable combination of posts in succession, only one will be indicated. And only *simultaneous* participation in two or more leadership functions will be listed.[4]

In the Catholic bloc, the following leaders occupied two or more top functions in their bloc organizations. When a leader's specific position in an organization is not stated, he was on its highest executive organ:

J. A. Middelhuis: Catholic labor union (chairman) + Catholic party M.P. in First Chamber + Catholic party executive committee

J. Zwanikken: Catholic labor union + Catholic party M.P. in Second Chamber

P. C. W. M. Bogaers: Catholic labor union + Catholic party M.P. in Second Chamber

P. M. H. van Boven: Catholic employers association (chairman) + Catholic party executive committee

Th. S. J. Hooij: Catholic retailers association (vice-chairman) + Catholic party M.P. in First Chamber + Catholic party executive committee

R. J. Nelissen: Catholic retailers association (secretary) + Catholic party M.P. in Second Chamber

C. G. A. Mertens: Catholic farmers association (chairman) + Catholic party M.P. in First Chamber

T. Brouwer: Catholic farmers association (secretary) + Catholic party M.P. in Second Chamber + Catholic party executive committee

C. J. van der Ploeg: Catholic farm workers union (chairman) + Catholic party M.P. in Second Chamber

---

[4] Furthermore, ties between the parties' parliamentary delegations and the external party organizations (which are common in many countries) are not listed, except when the person involved was also a leader of another bloc institution.

H. W. van Doorn: Catholic radio association (chairman) +
Catholic party M.P. in Second Chamber + Catholic party
executive committee

Th. Loerakker: Catholic radio association + Catholic labor
union

J. M. Peters: Catholic radio association + Catholic newspaper *De Nieuwe Limburger* (editor-in-chief) + Catholic
party M.P. in Second Chamber

W. P. G. Assmann: Catholic newspaper *Brabants Nieuwsblad* (editor-in-chief) + Catholic party M.P. in Second
Chamber

G. C. J. D. Kropman: Catholic newspaper *De Tijd-Maas-
bode* (chairman of the board of directors) + Catholic
party M.P. in First Chamber

J. J. Gielen: Catholic University of Nijmegen (professor) +
Catholic party M.P. in First Chamber

M. M. A. A. Janssen: Catholic Institute of Economics in
Tilburg (trustee) + Catholic party M.P. in Second Chamber

Th. L. M. Thurlings: State School of Agriculture in Wageningen (professor)—a Catholic counterpart does not
exist! + Catholic party M.P. in First Chamber

It is to be noted that the pattern of overlaps involves the
very top of the bloc leadership: chairmen, vice-chairmen,
etc. Connections with the church are not indicated. The
Catholic party and other Catholic organizations are not
organs of the church. Functionaries of the church do, however, occupy important positions in the Catholic lay organizations. For instance, Father L. J. C. Beaufort was a Catholic party representative in the Second Chamber from 1937
to 1946, in the First Chamber from 1948 to 1963, and also
a prominent member of the party executive committee. Catholic priests often sit on the governing boards of their bloc
organizations as spiritual advisers.

An examination of the leaders of Calvinist bloc organizations produces a similar list of multiple office holders. The names are different, of course, and there are two parties instead of one, but the over-all picture is much the same:

C. J. van Mastrigt: Protestant labor union (chairman) + Protestant radio association + Christian Historical M.P. in First Chamber + Christian Historical Union executive committee (vice-chairman)

C. van Nierop: Protestant labor union (secretary) + Anti-Revolutionary M.P. in Second Chamber

A. Borstlap: Protestant labor union + Anti-Revolutionary party executive committee

E. P. Verkerk: Protestant employers association + Anti-Revolutionary M.P. in Second Chamber

M. A. Geuze: Protestant employers association + Christian Historical Union executive committee

A. H. B. Breukelaar: Protestant employers association + Protestant retailers association

H. de Mooy: Protestant retailers association (chairman) + Anti-Revolutionary party executive committee

R. Zijlstra: Protestant farmers association (chairman) + Anti-Revolutionary party executive committee

H. W. Hielkema: Protestant farmers association + Christian Historical Union executive committee

H. Kikkert: Protestant farm workers union + Protestant radio association + Christian Historical M.P. in Second Chamber + Christian Historical Union executive committee

A. B. Roosjen: Protestant radio association (chairman) + Anti-Revolutionary M.P. in Second Chamber + Anti-Revolutionary party executive committee (vice-chairman)

G. A. Kieft: Protestant radio association (secretary) + Anti-Revolutionary M.P. in Second Chamber

D. van der Kwaak: Protestant radio association (treasurer) + Christian Historical Union executive committee

J. A. H. J. S. Bruins Slot: Anti-Revolutionary newspaper *Trouw* (editor-in-chief) + Anti-Revolutionary M.P. in Second Chamber

H. Algra: Protestant newspaper *Friesch Dagblad* (editor-in-chief) + Anti-Revolutionary M.P. in First Chamber + Anti-Revolutionary party executive committee

I. A. Diepenhorst: Calvinist Free University (professor) + Anti-Revolutionary M.P. in First Chamber

W. F. de Gaay Fortman: Calvinist Free University (professor) + Anti-Revolutionary M.P. in First Chamber + Anti-Revolutionary party executive committee

J. W. van Hulst: Calvinist Free University (professor) + Christian Historical M.P. in First Chamber

Again the highest bloc leaders are members of the interlocking directorates. The elite of the Anti-Revolutionary party is more deeply involved in other Protestant political and social organizations than those of the Christian Historical Union: a reflection of the former party's greater zeal, more efficient organization, and larger support from the voters—though the party was only slightly ahead of the Christian Historical Union in the 1963 elections. The occupancy of the Protestant labor-union chairmanship by the Christian Historical Union's Van Mastrigt lasted only a few years; both his predecessor, who held the post for over a decade, and his successor were Anti-Revolutionaries. It should also be noted that the above list of interlocking directorates in the Calvinist bloc, like the Catholic bloc's, includes *all* major institutions: not a single interest group, radio organization, or private university is excepted.

In the Socialist bloc the informal connections are equally strong. Employers, farmers, and retailers associations are absent from the list; they belong to the Liberal rather than the Socialist bloc. The following picture emerges:

D. Roemers: Socialist labor union (chairman) + Labor party M.P. in Second Chamber

A. H. Kloos: Socialist labor union (vice-chairman) + Labor party M.P. in First Chamber

C. W. van Wingerden: Socialist labor union (secretary) + Labor party M.P. in First Chamber

I. Baart: Socialist labor union + Labor party M.P. in Second Chamber

J. J. Kramer: Socialist labor union + Labor party M.P. in Second Chamber

S. van der Ploeg: Socialist farm workers union (chairman) + Labor party M.P. in First Chamber

H. Vredeling: Socialist farm workers union + Labor party M.P. in Second Chamber

J. A. W. Burger: Socialist radio association (chairman) + Labor party M.P. in Second Chamber + Labor party executive committee

J. B. Broeksz: Socialist radio association (secretary) + Labor party M.P. in First Chamber

C. van der Waerden: Socialist publishing company De Arbeiderspers (managing director)—publisher of *Het Vrije Volk* + Labor party M.P. in First Chamber

F. Schurer: Socialist newspaper *De Friese Koerier* (editor-in-chief) + Labor party M.P. in Second Chamber

J. P. Mazure: State Institute of Technology in Delft (professor) + Labor party M.P. in First Chamber

A. Querido: Municipal University of Amsterdam (professor) + Labor party M.P. in First Chamber

B. V. A. Röling: State University of Groningen (professor) + Labor party executive committee

I. Samkalden: State University of Leyden (professor) + Labor party M.P. in First Chamber + Labor Party executive committee·

S. A. Posthumus: State Institute of Technology in Eindhoven (trustee) + Labor party M.P. in Second Chamber

It is clear that, although the Socialists forswore self-containment in 1945 and severed their party's ties with the

Socialist labor union, informal connections among Socialist organizations by means of interlocking directorates have remained strong. In fact, the pattern of overlapping leadership looks much like those in the Catholic and Calvinist blocs.

For the Liberal bloc, the situation in the early 1960's was different. Even a thorough search could not unearth cases of overlap in all categories. In particular, such links were missing in the Liberal farmers association, radio organization, and newspapers. All these Liberal organizations—including the employers and retailers—use the epithet "general" rather than "Liberal," and the radio association (A.V.R.O.) emphatically avoids identification with the Liberals. Thus the fourth list is considerably shorter than the previous three:

G. C. van Dijk: Liberal employers association (secretary) + Liberal party executive committee

K. van der Pols: Liberal employers association + Liberal party executive committee (chairman)

C. A. Kammeraad: Liberal retailers association + Liberal party M.P. in Second Chamber

F. Portheine: Liberal retailers association + Liberal party M.P. in Second Chamber

H. J. Witteveen: State Institute of Economics in Rotterdam (professor) + Liberal party M.P. in First Chamber

In contrast to the other three blocs, the Liberals constitute a self-contained group not so much by choice as by necessity. They seek isolation less than the other three blocs but are forced into it by the isolationism of the others. The relatively low incidence of interlocking directorates in this bloc demonstrates its elite's weaker cohesion, but its leaders nonetheless form a set distinctly separate from the other three elites.[5]

The church affiliations of the four elites also follow the expected pattern. According to a survey of the religious com-

---

[5] The Liberal elite also has special ties with big business. See P. Vinke, *De maatschappelijke plaats en herkomst der directeuren en commissarissen van de open en daarmede vergelijkbare besloten naamloze vennootschappen* (Leyden: H. E. Stenfert Kroese, 1961).

position of the Second Chamber elected in 1967, all 42 Catholic party members belonged to the Catholic Church. All 27 members of the Anti-Revolutionary party and the Christian Historical Union belonged to the Reformed or Dutch Reformed churches: the latter were exclusively Dutch Reformed and the former were Reformed with only two exceptions. Of the 54 Socialists and Liberals in the Chamber, 26 (almost half) did not belong to any church, 20 belonged to the Dutch Reformed Church (presumably its liberal wing) or to minor dissenting churches, and only 6 were Catholic and 2 Reformed.[6]

A few more nuances must be added to the portrayal of the four elites. Not every major organization is rigidly tied to a bloc either formally or informally. There are exceptions, particularly in the Liberal camp but also in the other blocs. The national newspapers are the best example of the wide range from close dependence to complete independence. The three major Catholic, Socialist, and Calvinist papers are closely bloc-connected. *Het Parool*, however, is ideologically pro-Socialist but otherwise independent and often critical of the Labor party and the Socialist union and radio. Similarly, the Catholic *De Tijd* and the Liberal papers belong to their respective blocs but in an ideological rather than formal organizational sense. And the yellow press as well as Holland's largest political weekly (*Elsevier's Weekblad*) are stridently right-wing in their outlook but organizationally independent.[7]

These nuances modify but do not erase the picture of four rigidly separate elites leading the four blocs. The political

[6] Adapted from a survey in *Hervormd Nederland*, reported in *N.R.C. Overzeese Weekeditie*, Vol. 20, No. 47 (February 28, 1963), p. 7.

[7] Ties between newspapers and political leaders have been closer in the past. The trend started in the late nineteenth century and reached a peak in the early years of the twentieth century. See N. Cramer, *Parlement en pers in verhouding tot de overheid* (Leyden: H. E. Stenfert Kroese, 1958), pp. 168–176.

parties play the most significant role in tying the elites together. In virtually all cases of overlap, the party groups in
the First and Second chambers or the party executive committees figure prominently. Thus the political parties are the
central and most inclusive organs of the four blocs.[8] Perhaps
the most significant conclusion which emerges from the examination of interlocking directorates is that, though the
degree of overlap differs from bloc to bloc, it occurs only
within the bloc. Intrabloc overlap is the rule and *not a single
instance of overlap between different blocs can be found:* not
one Protestant union leader represents the Labor party in
parliament, not one leader of the Catholic employers belongs
to the Liberal party elite, and not one of the professors in
parliament is connected with the "wrong" university. The
only exception seems to be Catholic professor Thurlings of
the public School of Agriculture in Wageningen, but, as
noted above, the Catholic bloc does not have a similar school
of its own.[9]

The previous chapter showed that social cleavages are
deep but not altogether insurmountable at the mass level.
There are a few Anti-Revolutionaries who belong to the
Socialist union, a few practicing Catholics who vote for the
Liberal party, and so on. At the elite level such equivocation
does not occur. The bloc boundaries are clear and unmistakable.

THE DUTCH CASE AND PLURALIST THEORY

Is the Netherlands unique among Western
democracies in having such extraordinary divisions in its
social structure? Religious and class divisions are not un-

[8] See also I. Lipschits, "Partijbestuur en fractie," *Acta Politica*,
Vol. 1, Nos. 1–4 (1965–66), pp. 165–170.

[9] It should be noted that Thurlings was not the only Catholic
professor at a public university or institute of higher learning. His
case is exceptional because he was not just an individual Roman
Catholic but a representative of the Catholic party in the First
Chamber.

common elsewhere, of course. Class differences are present in all modern industrial societies, and religious differences, often compounded by a split between religious and anticlerical groups, are only a slightly less common feature. Elsewhere these divisions also give rise to different political allegiances and separate political and social structures for the different subcultural segments of the population. Directly church-related activities such as hospitals and charities are organized on more or less strict denominational lines almost everywhere. Similarly, private denominational schools exist nearly everywhere alongside public schools. Newspapers are often connected with political parties, though less frequently and less strongly in the United States, Britain, the Commonwealth democracies, Bonn Germany, and the Scandinavian countries, than elsewhere on the European continent. Party systems reflect religious and class cleavages, too. Class-based Labor, Socialist, or Communist parties are the rule rather than the exception, and religious parties—usually Christian Democratic parties—exist in all continental European democracies except Scandinavia. In the same countries we usually find labor unions split along religious and ideological lines: Catholic, Socialist, and sometimes Communist unions.[10]

One cannot claim, therefore, that Holland's situation is unique. But two factors make it particularly interesting in the context of pluralist theory. First, Holland's class and religious cleavages run deeper, the organization of its society on bloc lines is much more thorough, and the interpenetration of parties, interest groups, and communication media reaches much farther than in the Anglo-American and Scandinavian countries. It is a difference in degree, but clearly a very great difference. The difference between Holland and the other continental countries is less striking. Belgium, for instance, can be described as a country with three population

[10] See J. P. Kruijt, *Verzuiling* (Zaandijk: Heijnis, 1959), pp. 13–14.

groups similar to Holland's four blocs: Catholic, Socialist, and Liberal.[11] Austria, with its Catholic and Socialist *Lager*, is another example.

Second, though Dutch society is at least as much divided as other continental societies, it has sustained a stable and viable democratic system. This much cannot be claimed without major qualifications for Belgium, Austria, France, or Weimar Germany.

It is this combination of deep social cleavages and clearly viable democracy which makes Holland an eminently significant case for pluralist theory. It is a nation divided, but not one divided against itself. What can this case tell us about the conditions of stable and effective democracy?

[11] See Val R. Lorwin, "Conflict and Compromise in Belgian Politics" (unpublished paper presented at the annual meeting of the American Political Science Association, 1965); Lorwin, "Belgium: Religion, Class, and Language in National Politics," in Robert A. Dahl, ed., *Political Oppositions in Western Democracies* (New Haven: Yale University Press, 1966), pp. 147–187; and Lorwin, "Constitutionalism and Controlled Violence in the Modern State: The Case of Belgium" (unpublished paper presented at the annual meeting of the American Historical Association, 1965).

Chapter IV
VIABLE DEMOCRACY

Are we justified in using the Netherlands as an example of stable and effective democracy? Most observers would readily agree that there can be no serious disagreement on this question. But because the viability of the Dutch democratic system is a crucial element in the thesis of this study, it is important to subject it to a careful evaluation.

Both "democracy" and "stability" cannot be defined easily. We shall use these terms in the following sense: democracy means simply a system of government in which the people have the opportunity to select their own leaders. A *def.* stable democracy is one in which the capabilities of the system are sufficient to meet the demands placed upon it. This requires more than the maintenance of a stable order: problems, tensions, and conflicts should be resolved, and not be allowed to pile up. A healthy democracy is one characterized by gradual peaceful change or dynamic stability.[1] Does

[1] See David Easton, *A Systems Analysis of Political Life* (New

Dutch democracy satisfy this requirement? This question
will be explored in detail in later chapters, but as a prelimin-
ary step a number of gross indicators will be used to measure
the health of the system: negative indicators—the absence
of revolution, violence, and other signs of serious disaffection—and positive indicators—governmental stability and
constitutional continuity.

PEACEFUL CHANGE

The Dutch system of government did not
become fully democratic until 1918, the year of the first
elections under universal manhood suffrage. During the second half of the nineteenth century, Holland moved in the
direction of democracy. Parliamentarism—cabinet account-
ability to parliament—was established in 1868, and the
major constitutional revision which rendered the transition
toward strictly limited constitutional monarchy and full parliamentary democracy possible was achieved in 1848. In
evaluating the viability of Dutch democracy, the latter year
will be our starting point.

Since 1848, Holland has not experienced any civil wars,
rebellions, or attempts to upset the government by violent
means. It is significant that the major liberalization of the
constitution in 1848 was not the result of revolution. It was
achieved under the influence of revolutions elsewhere in
Europe, but in Holland itself a tense peace was maintained.
Other tensions were also resolved peacefully, along constitutional evolutionary paths. In 1853, the pope decided to
reestablish the Catholic episcopal hierarchy in the Netherlands—banned since the Reformation but legally admissible
once again under the religious-freedom clauses of the 1848
Constitution. This caused a storm of protest and agitation
(the so-called April Movement) which pitted Calvinists

York: John Wiley, 1965), pp. 17–25; and Easton, *A Framework for
Political Analysis* (Englewood Cliffs, N. J.: Prentice-Hall, 1965),
pp. 103–108.

against Liberals and Catholics. The Liberal cabinet fell and was replaced by a conservative government strongly supported by the Calvinists. But no action against the Catholic Church was taken, and tension gradually dissolved.[2] In 1878 a new crisis arose over the Education Act which strongly favored public over private schools. Together with the volatile issue of suffrage extension, it dominated Dutch politics for four decades. These major crises, which will be discussed more fully in a later chapter,[3] set Calvinists and Catholics against Liberals, and conservatives against progressives. The issues were allowed to remain unsettled for a long time but in the end a satisfactory solution was reached by constitutional methods.

The nationwide railroad strikes of 1903 came close to violence. The first phase was nonviolent and successful, and the railroad companies soon had to capitulate. The conservative government then proposed a law prohibiting strikes in public services, which was passed over the opposition of left-wing Liberals and Socialists. The railroad unions, more and more under the influence of anarchist elements, responded by calling a general strike against the law. It did not succeed, mainly because of the government's use of force; the military occupied all stations. But the moderates triumphed after all: the conservative government was defeated in 1905 by a coalition of the moderate left, and a new Socialist union was set up (the present N.V.V.) which soon lured away most of the anarchists' support.[4]

[2] W. J. van Welderen baron Rengers, *Schets eener parlementaire geschiedenis van Nederland van 1849 tot 1901* (4th ed., The Hague: Nijhoff, 1948), Vol. 1, pp. 87–109; P. J. Oud, *Honderd jaren, 1840–1940: Een eeuw van staatkundige vormgeving in Nederland* (Assen: Van Gorcum, 1954), pp. 41–52.

[3] See below, pp. 104–112.

[4] See Marinus M. Lourens, "Labor," in Bartholomew Landheer, ed., *The Netherlands* (Berkeley: University of California Press, 1943), pp. 194–196; H. Hoefnagels, *Een eeuw sociale problematiek: Van sociaal conflict naar strategische samenwerking* (Assen: Van Gorcum, 1957), pp. 107–110.

Another negative indicator of the viability of Dutch democracy is the weakness of political movements completely opposed to the existing democratic system. The Communist party never gained more than about 3 per cent of the vote before the Second World War. They gained respectability during the war because of their role in the anti-German resistance and the Soviet Union's participation on the allied side; in the first postwar elections they gained 10.6 per cent of the vote. But their support dwindled rapidly again: it was down to 4.8 per cent in 1956 and 3.6 per cent in 1967. The Dutch National Socialists did not attract much of a following either. They reached a peak of only 7.9 per cent of the total vote in the provincial elections of 1935, and received even less votes in the 1937 and 1939 elections: 4.2 and 3.9 per cent.

The Dutch Socialists have been free from anticonstitutional tendencies except in the very beginning. The only major exceptions were Socialist leader P. J. Troelstra's revolutionary words—but not deeds—in 1918 and the antimonarchical stand of the party; republicanism was dropped in the 1930's. The Socialists also disposed of the orthodox Marxists within their ranks at a very early date. At the 1909 party congress, a small group led by D. Wijnkoop was expelled from the party. This group later became the nucleus for the Communist party. The continued moderation of the Socialists is especially noteworthy because they were long kept from positions of power. In 1913 they were offered posts in a coalition cabinet with the Liberals, but declined. Later the parties of the right, dominant after 1918, refused to take them into the government, and they had to wait until 1939 before entering the cabinet—later than any other West European Socialist party.[5]

[5] H. Daalder, "Nationale politieke stelsels: Nederland," in L. van der Land, ed., *Repertorium van de sociale wetenschappen: Politiek* (Amsterdam: Elsevier, 1958), pp. 228–229.

STABILITY AND CONTINUITY

A positive indicator of the viability of Dutch democracy is the remarkable degree of cabinet stability. From 1848 to 1965, there were 47 different cabinets lasting an average of almost two and a half years. Mattei Dogan and Maria Scheffer-Van der Veen found, however, that the usually long duration of cabinets was not matched by an equally long life of individual ministers. From 1848 to 1956, 38 per cent of the ministers were in office less than two years and 77 per cent lasted less than four years. Only 23 per cent, or less than a fourth, stayed in office for more than four years. Another way of measuring the degree of ministerial stability is to look at the number of cabinets in which individual ministers participated. Of the 334 ministers from 1848 to 1956, 67 per cent served in only one cabinet, 18 per cent in two, and 15 per cent in three or more cabinets.[6]

The situation has improved since the establishment of full democracy in 1918. Table 18 shows the number of different cabinets and key ministers after 1848. The average duration

TABLE 18.   GOVERNMENT STABILITY, 1848-1965

(Number of *different* cabinets and key ministers)

Period	Cabinets	Prime ministers	Finance ministers	Ministers of internal affairs	Ministers of foreign affairs
1848–1868	11	9	8	10	12
1868–1918	15	15	18	17	16
1918–1945	12	4	8	6	5
1945–1965	9	5	5	6	6

[6] Mattei Dogan and Maria Scheffer-Van der Veen, "Le personnel ministériel hollandais (1848–1958)," *L'Année Sociologique*, 3rd series, 1957–1958, pp. 123–124. Twelve secretaries of state ("under-ministers") serving between 1949 and 1956 are also included among the 334 "ministers."

of cabinets after 1918 was 2.2 years compared with 2.7 years for the previous periods. But important cabinet posts tended to remain in the same hands. In the interwar period, there were only three different prime ministers, and only five during the twenty years after the Second World War, including the long reign of Prime Minister W. Drees from 1948 to 1958. Other key positions did not often change hands either. In some cases, the statistics exaggerate the changes in government. The Ministry of Foreign Affairs has been headed by six different ministers in the postwar period, but one man has been the dominant force for about two-thirds of that time: J. M. A. H. Luns. Luns became minister without portfolio in 1952 but actually concerned himself with foreign affairs. In 1956 he became minister of foreign affairs and it is not unlikely that his tenure will last into the 1970's.

It is true that Holland is known for its long cabinet crises. From 1878 to 1963, there were 34 crises with an average duration of about one and a half months.[7] In 1956 one lasted for almost four months, and the total number of days of crisis in the postwar period matches the record of the French Fourth Republic. But the number of crises is smaller and cabinets, once they are established after arduous negotiations, are much more stable.[8] It would be more accurate to speak of the long duration of cabinet formation than of "cabinet crises." They are not really crises, but periods in which the major parties are engaged in intense efforts of basic policy-making.

[7] Georg Geismann, *Politische Struktur und Regierungssystem in den Niederlanden*, Kölner Schriften zur Politischen Wissenschaft, Vol. 4 (Frankfurt am Main and Bonn, Athenäum Verlag, 1964), p. 289.
[8] See E. van Raalte, *Het Nederlandse Parlement* (The Hague: Staatsdrukkerij- en Uitgeverijbedrijf, 1958), pp. 49–54; H. Daalder, "Parties and Politics in the Netherlands," *Political Studies*, Vol. 3, No. 1 (February 1955), p. 8; Robert C. Bone, "The Dynamics of Dutch Politics," *Journal of Politics*, Vol. 24, No. 1 (February 1962), p. 36.

Finally, <u>constitutional continuity is evidence of the sta-</u><u>bility of the Dutch</u> governmental system. The present constitution—adopted in 1815—is one of the world's oldest. In 1848 it was drastically amended, and less sweeping changes were made repeatedly in later years. But the development from the enlightened despotism of King William I (1813–1840) to parliamentary democracy, universal suffrage, and the welfare state, took place within the framework of the old constitution. All major political problems facing the Dutch during the past century have been resolved peacefully and constitutionally. The only big blot on their record is their failure to withdraw from the colonial empire without bloodshed and severe damage to their national interest.

Democratic government has proved both legitimate and effective. In fact, Dutch politics appears to be not just healthy and stable, but decidedly dull and unexciting. This is perhaps the reason why political scientists have paid so little attention to it thus far, in spite of the fact that Holland is the largest (in terms of population) of the smaller West European democracies.

Chapter V

THE NARROW
NATIONAL CONSENSUS

The Netherlands cannot be called a consensual society, not even by the most generous stretch of the imagination. Consensus exists within each of the subcultures rather than among all four blocs. No state can exist without some degree of consensus on matters of fundamental concern, however, and Holland is no exception. Consensus can vary in degree (from complete agreement to complete disagreement) and in extent (covering all substantive and procedural values or none of these). In the Netherlands, both the degree and extent of political consensus are very limited, but one vitally important element of consensus is present: the desire to preserve the existing system. Each bloc tries to defend and promote its own interests but only within the confines of the total system and without the threat of secession or civil war. How can we account for this commitment to system maintenance among the diverse and mutually isolated blocs?

NATIONALISM

The most important factor behind this element of consensus is Dutch nationalism: the feeling of belonging to a common nation as well as to one's own bloc. The strength of this nationalism must not be exaggerated, but it certainly does exist.[1] National independence was achieved at a relatively early date, and feelings of nationalism can be traced back to the early stage of the struggle for independence: the end of the sixteenth century.[2] The separate Catholic, Calvinist, and secular subcultures also had their origin in this period, but the blocs did not become thoroughly organized until the nineteenth century. In other words, nationalism and the nation-state antedated by several centuries the outburst of organizational differentiation by the various subcultures.

The combination of national with bloc loyalty by the Calvinists is not hard to understand. Calvinism became almost synonymous with Dutch patriotism as a result of the war of independence which was a struggle against both Spanish rule as such and the Spanish attempt to re-impose Roman Catholicism on the Dutch. Calvinism became the dominant force in the Netherlands Republic, and Calvinists continued to enjoy a privileged position until the nineteenth century. The freethinking or secular bloc also had good reasons for national allegiance. Many of them had Calvinist origins and thus inherited patriotic feelings, and they were well repre-

[1] See also the data on national allegiance in Table 2 above (p. 22), and on the different interpretations of national history as a subject in elementary schools (pp. 52–53). The strong and near-unanimous Dutch support for the various schemes of European integration—much stronger than in the other five countries of the Europe of the Six—also suggests the relative weakness of Dutch nationalism.

[2] P. Geyl, "Godsdienst en nationaliteit in de Nederlanden," in *Studies en strijdschriften* (Groningen: Wolters, 1958), p. 5; J. Huizinga, "How Holland Became a Nation," in *Lectures on Holland* (Leyden: Sijthoff, 1924), p. 12.

sented especially among the better educated in the regent class. The French Revolution and the Batavian Republic propelled them to power in the nineteenth century, and as elsewhere nineteenth-century liberalism was closely identified with nationalism.

The Catholics were in a much less enviable position. The war of independence against Catholic Spain caused Roman Catholicism to be regarded as implying disloyalty. Catholic churches and services were banned in 1573 first as a temporary measure, but it later became a permanent prohibition. Catholics were also forbidden to assume public office and to establish their own schools. When the two largely Catholic southern provinces had been conquered by the forces of the Netherlands Republic, they did not become part of the seven United Provinces but were ruled as colonies and exploited economically.[3] It is surprising that this history of discrimination and denial of religious freedom and self-government did not turn the Catholics against the Dutch nation.

Instead, the Catholic minority always fought for emancipation *within* the nation. The main reason was that some degree of satisfaction of Catholic aspirations was not entirely precluded. During the days of the Netherlands Republic, Catholic churches and religious services were banned, but being a Roman Catholic was not a crime. In practice, private and covert Catholic worship was also condoned by the Protestant latitudinarians among the political rulers. And the general spirit was far from illiberal; after all, Holland became a sanctuary for Jews and other persecuted non-Calvinist minorities.[4] After the demise of the Dutch Republic, the Catholics found strong allies in the Liberals. In the liberal constitutions of 1798 and 1848, they received self-

[3] J. J. O. Goddijn, *Katholieke minderheid en protestantse dominant* (Assen: Van Gorcum, 1957), pp. 39–62.

[4] Pieter Geyl, "Liberty in Dutch History," *Delta*, Vol. 1, No. 3 (Autumn 1958), pp. 11–21; Johan Goudsblom, *Dutch Society* (New York: Random House, 1967), pp. 17–18.

government and religious freedom. Later when they sought public aid to private Catholic schools they entered an alliance with the Calvinists. At crucial times and on vital issues relief was usually obtainable, and the Catholic bloc did not become estranged from the Dutch nation.

Two other factors behind the existence of nationalistic feelings among Catholics and their lack of revolutionary and secessionist sentiments must be mentioned. First, although the two predominantly Catholic southern provinces are geographically close to the Flemings, whom they resemble in speech and religion, Dutch Catholics do not live exclusively in the South,[5] and even the South has long been economically interdependent with the Dutch state. The theoretical possibility of secession from Holland and union with their Belgian, and particularly their Flemish brothers, has never been seriously entertained by Dutch Catholics. Secondly, the doctrine of the Catholic Church does not condone revolution and secession, a factor of particular significance because Catholic political leadership in the nineteenth century was to greater extent in the hands of priests rather than of Catholic laymen. The following statement by J. A. Luyben, Catholic member of the Second Chamber, in 1840 illustrates the importance of church dogma:

> We Catholics do not want unrest in our beloved fatherland. *The doctrine of our church requires us to be obedient to the King and to abide by the law.* Our doctrine is replete with love for our fellow-men and love for our fatherland. We are attached to this beneficial doctrine heart and soul. We Catholics sincerely love our fatherland and in that love we match our Protestant fellow-citizens.[6]

In fact, Catholics have often been more emphatic and out-

[5] See above, p. 18.
[6] Quoted in H. J. G. Waltmans, *De Nederlandse politieke partijen en de nationale gedachte* (Sittard: Alberts, 1962), p. 51.

spoken about their loyalty and patriotism than other groups. H. J. A. M. Schaepman, the foremost leader of the Catholic bloc around the turn of the century, spoke in a similar vein: "In my whole life I have known only two loves, one for my fatherland and one for the mother-church."[7]

That strong bloc loyalties and interbloc rivalry and antagonism are not incompatible with national loyalty, should not be a surprising conclusion. It would be wrong to view national allegiance and bloc allegiance, system affect and subsystem affect, as constantly competing with each other. Group solidarities may be strong while overarching solidarities are *also* strong. Harry Eckstein states this point well when he argues that "division and cohesion in democracies do not belong to the world of zero sums. Nothing that makes either more considerable need diminish the other."[8]

NATIONAL SYMBOLS

Patriotism is reinforced by national symbols in addition to the symbols of the different blocs. They include the usual national symbols—flag, national anthem, national holidays—and the specifically Dutch national symbols of K.L.M. Royal Dutch Airlines (not just a business enterprise but the pride of the nation) and the massive project of land reclamation which is pursued with a determination and a cost to the taxpayer out of proportion to its economic and security benefits.[9] The most important symbol of national unity is the monarch, or, perhaps more accurately, the House of Orange. The Dutch monarchy is not very old; it dates from 1813. But the House of Orange has been closely identified

[7] Quoted *ibid.* See also Jonkheer G. van Benthem van den Bergh, "Nederland: Nationalisme op een zacht pitje," *Oost-West*, Vol. 5, No. 3 (March 1966), esp. pp. 95–97.

[8] Harry Eckstein, *Division and Cohesion in Democracy: A Study of Norway* (Princeton: Princeton University Press, 1966), p. 192.

[9] See Yehezkel Dror, "National Planning in the Netherlands," in Bertram M. Gross, ed., *National Planning: Purpose, Crisis, Power* (forthcoming).

with Dutch national history ever since William the Silent, the first Orange, who led the Dutch in the war of independence against Spain in the sixteenth century. Only Oranges have a right to the Dutch throne; a constitutional amendment passed in 1922 limited the succession to direct descendants of Queen Wilhelmina. The monarchs' political powers have become narrowly circumscribed, and their principal role now is a symbolic one.[10]

The House of Orange has not always been a truly national symbol. Until recently it was more closely identified with the Calvinist bloc than with the nation as a whole. The tie between Calvinism and the Oranges goes back to the war of independence when both were in the forefront of the struggle against Catholic Spain. More specifically, a close alliance between the House of Orange and the Calvinist bloc was created when Prince Maurice, son of William the Silent, led a coup d'état on their behalf in 1618 and 1619 against the "secular bloc" of that time, the more liberal and tolerant Arminian Protestants. It is significant, too, that the Calvinists, outraged at the re-establishment of the Catholic episcopal hierarchy in 1853, turned to King William III of Orange for redress—evidently regarding him more as the guardian of Calvinism than a symbol of national unity.

Conversely, the alliance between the House of Orange and the other three blocs has long been rather tenuous. The Liberals have never been antimonarchial, but their struggle for democratic reforms in the nineteenth century entailed drastic limitations on royal prerogatives and repeatedly brought them into conflict with the Orange monarchs. The Socialists were emphatically antimonarchical in their early

[10] Except in the extraordinary case of Queen Wilhelmina's dominant political role in the Dutch government-in-exile in London during the Second World War. See L. de Jong's address "Koningin Wilhelmina in Londen, 1940–1945" to the Royal Dutch Academy of Sciences on February 14, 1966, published in *Mededelingen der Koninklijke Nederlandse Academie van Wetenschappen, Afdeling Letterkunde*, Nieuwe Reeks, Vol. 29, No. 2 (1966).

years. The first major Socialist leader, F. J. Domela Nieu-
wenhuis, was prosecuted, convicted, and imprisoned for
lèse-majesté in 1887. In 1894, the program of the new Social
Democratic Labor party did not formally include the abolition of the monarchy—William III had died in 1890, and
his successor Queen Wilhelmina was only fourteen years old
—but the Socialists remained opposed to the monarchy. In
1909, when Princess Juliana was born, and again after the
First World War, Socialist leader P. J. Troelstra publicly
made scathing remarks about the monarchy. And for many
years the Socialist members of parliament refused to attend
the Queen's speech from the throne at the start of the annual
session of parliament.[11] They abandoned their antimonarchical stand in the 1930's, however.

For the Catholics, allegiance to a Protestant royal house
presents special problems. The 1814 constitution specified
that the monarch had to be a Protestant, but this provision
was deleted in the 1815 constitution drawn up after Holland's union with Belgium. For more than a century and a
half, therefore, the constitution has been silent on the question of the monarchs' religion, but they have nonetheless all
been members of the Dutch Reformed Church. Accepting a
traditionally Protestant king or queen cannot be a foregone
conclusion for Catholics; even more difficult to accept is the
Calvinist reluctance to envisage any different arrangement.
In 1964 this issue became critical when Princess Irene—
second in line for the succession to the throne—converted
to Roman Catholicism and married a Spanish Catholic
nobleman. In a public-opinion poll conducted in February
1964, people were asked about their attitudes toward the
possibility of having a Catholic king or queen. Only a minority (30 per cent) expressed a negative viewpoint, but the
responses were sharply different among the different blocs.

[11] P. J. Oud, *Honderd jaren, 1840–1940: Een eeuw van staatkundige vormgeving in Nederland* (Assen: Van Gorcum, 1954), pp.
187–188, 287.

Supporters of the Catholic party were overwhelmingly positive on this question: only 1 per cent expressed disapproval.
Opposition to a Catholic monarch was considerable among
Socialists (28 per cent) and Liberals (47 per cent). Supporters of the Protestant parties disapproved in very large
numbers: 68 per cent. Should a monarch abdicate if he becomes a Roman Catholic? None of the Catholic party supporters, but 29 per cent of the Socialists, 30 per cent of the
Liberals, and almost half (46 per cent) of the supporters of
the Protestant parties thought he should.[12]

Cabinet and parliament declined to give the constitutionally required approval to Irene's marriage, thereby excluding
her from succession to the throne. The official reason was
not Irene's conversion or her marriage to a Catholic, but her
husband's—rather dubious—claim to the Spanish throne
and his involvement in Spanish politics, regarded as incompatible with the proper role of a consort to a future Dutch
queen. The acceptability of a Catholic monarch was not
faced squarely, therefore. And many Catholics continued
to feel perturbed about their compatriots' opposition to a
Catholic king or queen. The Catholic newspaper *De Tijd*
called the royal family the "symbol of national unity" in
early 1964 after the announcement of Princess Irene's conversion, but a few weeks later the same paper had the following bitter editorial comment on Irene's exclusion from
the throne:

> We may be told ten times over that religion does not exclude
> anyone from succession to the throne, but it is a great pity
> that the rare occasion actually to prove this contention has
> now been lost. . . .
> No, what is done cannot be undone. But we regret that the
> most important question that was raised threatens to remain
> unanswered: the question of the true status of Dutch Catholics
> in the year 1964. Have they been living in "a fool's paradise"

[12] Nederlands Instituut voor de Publieke Opinie, *Bericht No. 986*
(March 13, 1964), and *Bericht No. 987* (March 16, 1964).

until now, unaware of the real opinion of their fellow-citizens
who still regard them as a foreign element in a Protestant
nation?[13]

During the Second World War, which the royal family
spent in exile in England and Canada, the monarchy became a truly national symbol for the first time. Soon after
the beginning of the German occupation in 1940, there
were widespread patriotic and anti-German demonstrations,
taking place, significantly, on June 29, the birthday of Prince
Bernhard. The royal house became even more popular later
during the same year. Almost everyone began to listen to
"Radio Orange," a fifteen-minute broadcast in the Dutch
language from England, and especially Queen Wilhelmina's
speeches were a source of inspiration to occupied Holland.[14]
The Nazis deliberately attempted to destroy the popularity
of the House of Orange, but this effort had the opposite
effect.[15]

Since then the royal house has been through a number of
storms, including Queen Juliana's controversial involvement
with faith healer Greet Hofmans, Princess Irene's conversion
and marriage, and, most recently, Crown Princess Beatrix's
marriage to Claus von Amsberg, a German with a record of
membership in the Hitler Youth and service in the *Wehr-
macht*. These and other minor irritations have weakened the
monarchy but its popularity has not been destroyed. Even
the strong and widely publicized protests against Beatrix's
marriage were restricted to a small minority. According to
two public opinion polls in October 1965, parliamentary

[13] *De Tijd* (January 29, February 10, 1964), quoted in Dick
Schaap and Bert Pasterkamp, *De zaak Irene* (Amsterdam: ABC-
Boeken, 1964), pp. 65, 137.

[14] Werner Warmbrunn, *The Dutch under German Occupation:
1940–1945* (Stanford: Stanford University Press, 1963), pp. 104–
105.

[15] Amry Vandenbosch and Samuel J. Eldersveld, *Government of
the Netherlands* (Lexington: Bureau of Government Research, University of Kentucky, 1947), p. 84.

approval of the marriage—without which Beatrix would have lost her right to the throne—was favored by about 73 per cent of the Dutch people and opposed by only 12 or 13 per cent.[16]

Overt republicanism remains weak. Only two splinter parties (the Communists and Pacifist Socialists) officially espouse the republican cause, and, according to an early 1964 poll, only 8 per cent of the Dutch people favored a republic compared with 86 per cent who supported the retention of the monarchy. Loyalty to the monarchy is strong among all major groups of the population with only slight variations: as expected, support for republicanism is lowest among voters favoring the Protestant parties (4 per cent) and somewhat higher among Labor party, Catholic party, and Liberal party adherents (8, 9, and 13 per cent respectively).

It is more difficult to gauge the depth of commitment to the monarchy, but it seems clear that the many upheavals which have rocked the Dutch royal house in recent years, have not made its position more secure. A survey conducted in July 1965, after Beatrix's controversial engagement had been announced, found that republicanism was not much stronger than a year and a half earlier (9 per cent favored a republic compared with the earlier 8 per cent), but support for the monarchy was down from 86 per cent to 74 per cent. Many more people had become uncertain.[17] Yet another poll, in September 1966, found a further decrease in support for the monarchy (71 per cent) and an increase in republican sentiment (15 per cent).[18]

Many Dutchmen may have doubts about the monarchy without necessarily joining republican ranks, and may con-

[16] Nederlands Instituut voor de Publieke Opinie, *Bericht No. 1079* (November 8, 1965).

[17] N.I.P.O., *Bericht No. 988* (March 17, 1964), *Bericht No. 1061* (July 15, 1965).

[18] "Politiek in Nederland: 3," *Revu* (December 31, 1966), p. 30.

tinue to be monarchists not on sentimental grounds but rather because of the absence of preferable alternatives. A clear
example of such an attitude appears in a letter by G. M.
Nederhorst, chairman of the Labor party delegation in the
Second Chamber. In this private letter, published without his
approval, Nederhorst was very critical of the present monarch and her most likely successor: "Wilhelmina was the
last queen who performed her task with an iron devotion to
duty. Juliana succeeds less well (e.g. the Hofmans affair),
and the heavy demands of the monarchy are completely un-
congenial to Beatrix." But the monarchy should be retained
since a republican form of government would have even
more distasteful consequences, according to this Socialist
leader: "A Holland headed by someone like Juliana or
Beatrix—firmly controlled by government and parliament—
is preferable to a Dutch republic headed by someone like
[the more popular than competent Catholic party leaders]
De Quay or Luns, because that is what we would get."[19]

Ernest Renan, speaking in 1882, emphasized the strong
link between Dutch nationalism and the House of Orange:
"Holland . . . entered into a close bond of marriage with the
House of Orange, and would run serious risks, should this
union ever be endangered."[20] As one of the few integrating
forces in Dutch society, the royal house performs an undeni-
ably vital function, but the "close bond of marriage" is by no
means so strong as to be indissoluble.

CROSSCUTTING LINKS

An important factor which does not provide
a common bond but at least mitigates the effects of the poor

[19] Quoted in *N.R.C. Overzeese Weekeditie*, Vol. 19, No. 29 (October 26, 1965), p. 4.
[20] Ernest Renan, "What Is a Nation?" in Alfred Zimmern, ed.,
Modern Political Doctrines (London: Oxford University Press,
1939), p. 193. See also N. Scheps, *Kontakt en kortsluiting tussen
vorst, regering en volk* (Kampen: J. H. Kok, 1964), esp. chap. 10.

integration of Dutch society, is the pattern of basic social cleavages. Religious and class lines sharply separate the four subcultural blocs from each other, but it is important to recognize that these cleavages do not coincide. It is not true, for instance, that Calvinists belong mainly to the middle class and Catholics to the working class. Each religious group con-

TABLE 19. RELIGION AND SOCIOECONOMIC STATUS
(In per cent)

Religion	(Number)	A (high)	B	C	D (low)
Catholic (regular)	(388)	8	34	53	5
Catholic (irregular)	(105)	13	24	49	14
Reformed	(157)	7	40	45	8
Dutch Reformed (regular)	(151)	8	41	41	11
Dutch Reformed (irregular)	(351)	5	34	52	9
Other religions	(56)	9	36	48	7
No religion	(361)	7	33	47	12
Catholic bloc	(388)	8	34	53	5
Secular bloc	(873)	7	33	49	11
Calvinist bloc	(308)	7	41	43	9
Total sample	(1597)	8	35	49	9

tains substantial numbers of both workers and middle-class people.

In fact, religious and class lines in Holland run at right angles to each other. If the class cleavage is represented as a horizontal line, the religious cleavages are almost perfectly vertical lines. Tables 19 and 20 show the relationship between religion and two indicators of class: the socioeconomic status of the respondents as assigned by the interviewers, and income. The class composition of each bloc is virtually identical to the class composition of the population as a whole regardless of whether class is measured in terms of income or in terms of socioeconomic status.

TABLE 20.   RELIGIOUS BLOCS AND INCOME
(In per cent)

Income (in thousands of guilders)	Bloc			
	Catholic (389)	Secular (873)	Calvinist (308)	Total (1,600)
More than 15	5	6	5	6
12–15	5	5	6	5
9.6–12	10	11	9	11
7.8–9.6	14	13	16	13
7.2–7.8	7	9	7	8
6.6–7.2	13	14	10	13
5.4–6.6	11	10	12	11
4.2–5.4	2	5	5	4
Less than 4.2	8	11	10	10
Don't know	24	16	20	19

The only qualification that must be made in this respect concerns the social position of the Roman Catholic bloc. For centuries Catholics were subject to systematic discrimination, and, in particular, were excluded from all governmental jobs. Even fairly recently, they held a disproportionately small share of the functions of prestige and political power. In

1871, only 6.5 per cent of the top echelon of civil servants in the ministries in The Hague were Catholic. There were only two Catholics among the 220 professors (not counting the professors of Protestant theology) at the Dutch universities in 1900. And it was not until 1918 that a Catholic became prime minister. Comparatively few Catholics received a university education—the principal avenue to prestige functions. In 1900, only 7.1 per cent of all university students were Catholic.[21]

This situation has improved considerably although even today Roman Catholics do not quite have their "fair share" of high functions. For instance, they had 21.9 per cent of the professorships in the mid-fifties: up from one per cent in 1900, but low compared with the 35 to 40 per cent share of Catholics in the total working population. At the same time, enrollment of Catholic students at the universities was 27.3 per cent of the total compared with an estimated 40 per cent of Catholic youth in the 18 to 20 year age range. And from 1871 to 1951, the percentage of Catholics among high civil servants increased from 6.5 to no more than 12 per cent.[22] On the other hand, the prime ministership is not only open to Catholics, but the Catholic party now clearly has the first claim to this post and feels fully entitled to it.

The apparent persistence of anti-Catholic discrimination can be explained largely as the effect of past discriminatory attitudes and practices rather than by their intentional

[21] M. Matthijssen, *De intellectuele emancipatie der katholieken* (Assen: Van Gorcum, 1958), p. 35. H. Verwey-Jonker claims that the percentage was even smaller: 1.5 per cent. See "De emancipatiebewegingen," in A. N. J. den Hollander, et al., eds., *Drift en koers: Een halve eeuw sociale verandering in Nederland* (Assen: Van Gorcum, 1962), p. 107.

[22] For the sources of these figures and further details, see: Matthijssen, pp. 30–39, 85–90; A. van Braam, *Ambtenaren en bureaukratie in Nederland* (The Hague: Excelsior, 1957), pp. 237–252; Van Braam, "Sociale herkomst en mobiliteit van ambtenaren," in F. van Heek and G. Kuiper, eds., *Sociale stijging en daling in Nederland* (Leyden: H. E. Stenfert Kroese, 1958), pp. 234–239.

continuation today. According to A. van Braam, most top
echelon bureaucrats are over forty years old and university-
educated. Therefore, considering the low university enrollments of Catholics during the past thirty or forty years, one
could not expect to find more than 15 or 20 per cent Catholics among the high civil servants in 1954, and their 14.4
per cent actual share of the group of about 1,200 top bureaucrats in 1954 was not severely disproportional. An additional factor which explains the impression of persistent discrimination is the geographical concentration of Catholics in the
southern provinces and the location of the two Catholic institutes of higher learning in the same area. New civil servants for the national governmental apparatus are recruited
primarily in The Hague and the western provinces where
non-Catholics are more strongly represented and therefore
more likely to seek entry into public administration.[23]

The basic fact remains nonetheless that the religious and
class lines are crosscutting cleavages. In this respect, the
Dutch situation may be compared with Switzerland where the
religious and linguistic dividing lines cut across each other,
and contrasted with the less fortunate case of Canada where
these lines coincide and constitute a single deep cleavage.
Such a comparison also calls attention to the fact that although Holland is a plural society, it is not divided by a serious controversy over language. Dutch is the language spoken
by the overwhelming majority of the people. A different language—Frisian—is spoken in the province of Friesland, but
the Frisians are few in number and most of them are bilingual.
There are many dialects. Of these, the southern accent is of
some importance in this context because it is one of the out-
ward signs of belonging to the Catholic bloc, at least for
those Catholics originating in the two overwhelmingly Catholic southern provinces.

[23] Van Braam, *Ambtenaren en bureaukratie*, p. 249; F. van Heek,
Het geboorte-niveau der Nederlandse Rooms-Katholieken (Leyden:
H. E. Stenfert Kroese, 1954), pp. 133–139.

The perpendicularity of class and religious cleavages does not necessarily or logically lead to unity. After all, when one cuts a pie crosswise one gets four separate pieces rather than a single whole pie! Crosscutting divisions may simply increase social fragmentation.[24] This analogy is quite revealing in the case of Holland although it is only partly applicable. One might hypothesize that the twofold division of class (middle vs. working class) cutting across the threefold religious division (Catholic vs. Calvinist vs. secular) would result in six separate segments. In some instances these six are clearly discernible. In the labor-relations field six groups confront each other: three labor unions and three employers associations. Also, as discussed in Chapter II, the major newspapers fit the sixfold pattern rather closely. The Socialist and Liberal blocs are perfectly bounded by these dividing lines. But here the analogy ends. The two other blocs *do* cut across a major cleavage: both the Catholic and Calvinist blocs are separated from other groups by religious cleavages, but they are not divided much further by class differences. The big Catholic and Protestant political parties are clearly not class parties. Class consciousness and antagonisms do exist within these blocs but they are subordinated to the need for religious unity. From this point of view, one can maintain that the Catholic and Calvinist blocs, in spite of their mutual isolation and self-containment, are not entirely homogeneous and not completely devoid of crosscutting internal divergence. We shall return to the significance of this pattern later.

One other important social institution cuts across a basic cleavage: the Dutch Reformed Church. It serves as a link between the Calvinist and secular blocs. The church has clearly discernible orthodox and liberal wings but these have remained united in a single organization. Furthermore, the General Synod, the highest governing organ of the church, has vigorously opposed the division of Dutch society into

[24] See Eckstein, *Division and Cohesion in Democracy*, pp. 73–75.

self-contained blocs, especially after the Second World War.
For instance, in a pastoral letter in 1955 the Synod emphasized the importance of the basic antithesis between the
forces of good and evil, "between the dominion of Christ and
the powers of darkness." But, the Synod warned, this antithesis "does not, in general, coincide with the cleavage between the aspirations and organizations of the Christians and
those of the non-Christians in the present era." And in sharp
contrast to the Catholic episcopal decree of 1954, the Synod
argued against the withdrawal of Protestants into separate
Protestant organizations: "Choosing a particular political
party is a matter for the faith and conscience of the individual. . . ." If a Protestant or other political party should ask
for the voter's allegiance in the name of God or Christ, then
"the Church would have to brand this claim as a vain use of
the Lord's Name in the sense of the Third Commandment."[25]

STABLE DEMOCRACY: OTHER HYPOTHESES

Other hypotheses have often been advanced
to account for the viability and consensual politics of some
democratic systems and the weaknesses of others. These must
be examined briefly in the context of Dutch politics. The first
hypothesis establishes a relationship between stages of economic development and the incidence of democracy. Lipset
states: "Perhaps the most common generalization linking
political systems to other aspects of society has been that democracy is related to the state of economic development. The
more well-to-do a nation, the greater the chances that it will
sustain democracy."[26] Holland can undoubtedly be classified
among the modern, developed, industrialized, and well-to-do

[25] Generale Synode van de Nederlandse Hervormde Kerk, *Christen-zijn in de Nederlandse samenleving* (The Hague: Boekencentrum,
1955), pp. 10, 19, 22–23. See also J. P. Kruijt, *Verzuiling* (Zaandijk:
Heijnis, 1959), pp. 17–18.
[26] Seymour Martin Lipset, *Political Man: The Social Bases of
Politics* (Garden City, N.Y.: Doubleday, 1960), pp. 48, 50.

nations, but it is far from the most outstanding example. On most indicators of wealth, industrialization, and urbanization, Holland ranks relatively low compared with other West European and Anglo-American states. For instance, among the thirteen European and English-speaking nations which Lipset classifies as "stable democracies" Holland ranks twelfth in G.N.P. per capita. Only Ireland ranks lower on this general indicator of wealth.[27] The Dutch case does not provide especially strong evidence for the economic explanation of viable democracy, therefore. And the argument that Holland's advanced state of economic development as a factor predisposing toward democracy can counteract the serious divisive forces in Dutch society, cannot be validly maintained.

More relevant than the *state* of economic development may *H* be the *rate* of economic development, on the assumption that democracy is best sustained by a citizenry confident of improving or at least maintaining their economic lot. After about 1950, Holland has shared in the remarkable West European economic growth and prosperity. The resulting widespread contentment and optimism is indicated by the drastic decline of interest in emigration. An opinion poll in 1948 found that about a third of the Dutch people wanted to leave Holland in order to build a new future overseas; in 1962 only 12 per cent expressed such an interest.[28] Periods of high economic growth have been relatively rare, however. During the second half of the nineteenth century, the annual growth rate was not much more than 1 per cent, barely higher than the growth of the population. Around 1900 it climbed to a bare 2 per cent. In the 1920's the rate of growth was sometimes higher than 4 per cent, but this period of rapid expansion was

[27] Based on the 1957 figures reported in Bruce M. Russett, et al., *World Handbook of Political and Social Indicators* (New Haven: Yale University Press, 1964), p. 155.
[28] Nederlands Instiuut voor de Publieke Opinie, *Bericht No. 907* (September 4, 1962).

followed by a decade and a half of depression and war. In
1959 the growth rate for the first time exceeded the 5 per
cent mark.[29]

Another widely accepted proposition is that stable and viable democracy depends on a history of gradual political development. England is usually considered the model of gradualism. One important aspect is the rate of democratization,
that is, the extension of the franchise. If mass participation
comes about in a gradual and evolutionary way, the electorate
is likely to be effectively socialized into participant roles and
introduced to democratic norms and practices. This hypothesis also fails as an explanation for the viability of the Dutch
democratic system. The right to vote was extended much
more rapidly than in England. The 1832 Reform Act resulted
in an increase of the number of eligible voters from 5 to 7.1
per cent of the total adult population in Britain. In Holland
the first extension of the franchise did not occur until 1887;
until that year the percentage of eligible voters was approximately the same as in England *before* the Reform Act, more
than half a century earlier. Once the first step was taken,
however, the franchise was extended very rapidly; universal
suffrage was adopted in 1919—compared with 1928 in Britain. In short, the process of democratization that took from
1832 to 1928 in England, nearly a full century, took only
slightly more than thirty years (1887–1919) in the Netherlands.

Gradualism may also be interpreted more broadly. In this
sense, gradual political development refers to the absence of
major political upheavals and revolutions in the development
toward democracy. England and France are usually represented as the extremes on opposite poles. In this respect, Holland can indeed be classified among the gradualists. In fact,
Holland is almost unique in that it has avoided any sustained
period of absolutism (with the sole exceptions of the Napo-
leonic era and the Second World War) since the attainment

[29] J. Pen and P. J. Bouman, "Een eeuw van toenemende welvaart,"
in Den Hollander, et al., *Drift en koers*, p. 92.

of independence in the seventeenth century. On the other hand, the argument which relates the viability of democracy to its evolutionary development begs the most crucial question. It fails to explain the reason why it was possible for a particular country to achieve democracy along evolutionary paths—which is probably also the most important reason for the persistence of a viable democracy. It fails to link cause and effect, but rather posits two effects without specifying the fundamental cause.

The process of industrialization and the rise of an industrial working class also occurred at a rather fast pace. As Lipset states, one of the factors to which the moderation of British politics is often attributed is that "its period of rapid industrialization occurred before the emergence of socialist movements."[30] In Holland the industrial revolution did not start until about 1870, considerably later than in its neighbors England, France, Belgium, and Germany.[31] And a large industrial proletariat did not develop until the end of the century, long after the establishment of Socialist movements throughout Europe. Neither did Holland have a strong nobility which could serve as a buffer between the middle and lower classes and a protector of workers' rights. Schumpeter argues that the persistent influence of such a nobility throughout the period of industrialization in England and Germany, unlike the situation in a country like France, had a moderating and stabilizing effect.[32] Holland has been a bourgeois nation for centuries with only a relatively minor and weak aristocratic element, although the nineteenth century *grande*

[30] Seymour Martin Lipset, "Political Cleavages in 'Developed' and 'Emerging' Polities," in Erik Allardt and Yrjö Littunen, eds., *Cleavages, Ideologies and Party Systems: Contributions to Comparative Political Sociology*, Transactions of the Westermarck Society, Vol. 10 (Helsinki, 1964), p. 26.

[31] See Pen and Bouman, pp. 88–91; H. Hoefnagels, *Een eeuw sociale problematiek: Van sociaal conflict naar strategische samenwerking* (Assen: Van Gorcum, 1957), p. 3.

[32] Joseph Schumpeter, *Capitalism, Socialism and Democracy* (3rd ed., New York: Harper & Brothers, 1950), pp. 134–139.

bourgeoisie itself often behaved like a parvenu aristocracy.[33]

Closely related to the hypothesis of gradual development is a third hypothesis which emphasizes the importance of

staggered development. The stability of a democratic system depends on its ability to resolve its major problems before new ones arise. In particular, to quote Lipset once again, "if the issues of religion, citizenship, and 'collective bargaining' are allowed to accumulate, they reinforce each other, and the more reinforced and correlated the sources of cleavage, the less likelihood for political tolerance."[34] This is exactly what happened in Holland around the turn of the century. During a relatively short period, from 1878 to 1917, all three of these crucial issues reached the boiling point. The religious issue revolving around the question of state aid to religious schools was fought in this period. The struggle to extend the suffrage took place at the same time. And as a result of the late arrival of the industrial revolution, the question of the workers' right to organize and bargain collectively also coincided with the other two basic issues. This period of turmoil will be discussed in greater detail later, but it is abundantly clear that Holland does not fit the staggered-development hypothesis.

The fourth hypothesis concerns the geographical distribution of the population in a plural society. Lipson states that if a minority is geographically concentrated and forms the majority within a certain region, "their physical proximity to one another and their control over a territorial area may increase their separatist feeling and their potency." The Catholic, Calvinist, and secular blocs all have their own geograph-

---

[33] Hans Daalder, "Parties, Elites, and Political Developments in Western Europe," in Joseph LaPalombara and Myron Weiner, eds., *Political Parties and Political Development* (Princeton: Princeton University Press, 1966), pp. 55–56; Daalder, "The Netherlands: Opposition in a Segmented Society," in Robert A. Dahl, ed., *Political Oppositions in Western Democracies* (New Haven: Yale University Press, 1966), pp. 196–197.

[34] Lipset, *Political Man*, p. 89.

ical strongholds. This is particularly true for the Roman Catholics; nationally they are a minority of about 40 per cent, but in the two southern provinces they constitute about 90 per cent of the population. Furthermore, Lipson says, such a minority "may receive reinforcement from others outside who belong to the same race or religion, or speak the same language. If the external sympathizers form a large and powerful bloc, and if they control the government of an important state, the minority that receives their backing may feel emboldened to resist the majority of their own society."[35] This condition applies only partly to the Dutch Catholic bloc. They are geographically close to the Flemings who have the same religion and speak the same language. But, though not a numerical minority, the Flemings have long been in a politically minor position and certainly have not controlled the government of a powerful state. In any case, Dutch Catholics have never engaged in any significant separatist movements despite their geographical concentration and their propinquity to the Flemings.

We must also consider the possibility that mutually reinforcing social cleavages may be mitigated to some extent by crosscutting divisions created by the governmental structure. Lipset argues: "If crosscutting bases of cleavage make a more vital democracy, it follows that, all other factors being constant, two-party systems are better than multi-party systems, that the election of officials on a territorial basis is preferable to proportional representation, and federalism is superior to a unitary state."[36] Similarly, the German sociologist Georg Simmel states: "Electoral procedures based on territorial units are . . . precisely the technique for the organic integration of the whole."[37] Lipset does not claim, of course,

[35] Leslie Lipson, *The Democratic Civilization* (New York: Oxford University Press, 1964), p. 92. See also above, pp. 18, 81.

[36] Lipset, *Political Man*, p. 90.

[37] Georg Simmel, *Conflict and the Web of Group Affiliations*, trans. Kurt H. Wolff and Reinhard Bendix (Glencoe: The Free Press, 1955), p. 194.

that these three conditions are indispensable for democracy, and he cites the example of democratic Sweden where none of the three conditions are present. The Dutch system of government does even less to encourage crosscutting cleavages by constitutional means. It is a unitary, not a federal state. The electoral system is one of the most meticulous forms of proportional representation with the entire country serving as the electoral district; a party needs as little as two-thirds of one per cent of the popular vote in order to gain a seat in the Second Chamber. And Holland has always had a multi-party system, with no less than ten parties represented in the 1963–1967 session of the Second Chamber, and eleven from 1967 on.

These five hypotheses, though they enjoy a prima facie credibility and may be true in many other cases, do not offer valid explanations of the viability of Dutch democracy. They were not discussed here in an attempt to disprove them, but only to demonstrate that the hypothesized factors conducive to stable and effective democracy are by and large absent in Holland and do not serve as countervailing agents which mitigate the effects of mutually reinforcing cleavages.

Two other hypotheses offer partly applicable reasons for democratic stability in the Netherlands. First, we have a whole series of propositions, expounded especially by Rousseau, which establish relationships between a country's size and the nature of its politics. Holland's population of about 13 million exceeds those of the other smaller European democracies, but is still a relatively small population by world standards; its territory is very limited indeed—about half the size of West Virginia—and it is the most densely populated country in the world. All these factors, according to Rousseau, should give such a country a particularly suitable environment for strong democracy because its society is likely to be cohesive: "Every extension of the social tie means its relaxation." In a large country, "the government [has] less vigour and promptitude for securing the observance of the laws, preventing nuisances, correcting abuses, and guarding against seditious undertakings begun in distant places; the people has less affection for its rulers, whom it never sees, for its country, which, to its eyes, seems like the world, and for its fellow citizens, most of whom are unknown to it. The same laws cannot suit so many diverse provinces with different customs."[38]

But Rousseau's assumption that a small, densely populated country is likely to be highly homogeneous and to have effective social communication, clearly does not fit the Dutch case. A different hypothesis linking size with stability is much more plausible. If we view the political stability of a democratic polity in terms of its capability to deal effectively with the problems confronting it, a small democracy has an inherent advantage in that it is less likely to lead an active foreign policy and to have grave burdens placed upon it in the form of difficult foreign policy choices. Holland followed a strict neutrality policy until the Second World War. The only international problem of more than local importance in which the Netherlands later had a significant, though not decisive, influence was the Dutch conflict with Indonesia from 1945 to 1949. This question was mentioned before as one with which the Dutch were unable to deal satisfactorily. It also produced serious strains in Dutch domestic politics, similar in nature but to an even greater extent than the internal political tensions in the United States over the Vietnam issue. The advantage which a small democracy may derive from its relative noninvolvement in international questions should not be underestimated, therefore. Even the Fourth French Republic, with all its shortcomings, might still be in existence today if it had not been for the essentially external question of Algeria.

Secondly, Harry Eckstein's proposition that stable democ-

---

[38] Jean Jacques Rousseau, *The Social Contract*, trans. G. D. H. Cole (New York: E. P. Dutton, 1950), pp. 44, 45; see also Book 3, chap. 8.

racy requires "considerable resemblance" or "congruence" between governmental patterns of authority and social patterns of authority "particularly in those segments of society which impinge directly on government,"[39] and Gabriel Almond and Sidney Verba's related proposition that stability depends on the degree of "congruence/incongruence between political structure and culture,"[40] both appear to fit the Dutch situation well. Dutch political structure is highly elitist and, therefore, congruent with Dutch political culture which is highly deferential. A later chapter will analyze the role of deferential attitudes in greater detail, and will point out that, in this respect, the blocs are remarkably similar.[41] It is important to raise this point here, not only because of its relevance to the theories of congruence, but also because it demonstrates that the Dutch national consensus, characterized earlier as a narrow and limited consensus, does include agreement on this set of crucial procedural norms.

We are still faced, however, with the problem of explaining the stability of Dutch democracy in spite of the wide divergence in *substantive* values among the subcultures. It will be argued that deference makes an indispensable contribution to the process of reconciling divergent substantive goals. The deferential pattern of authority, both social and governmental, does provide an explanation of the stability of Dutch democracy but only in an indirect way, or, to put it differently, only as one component of a larger, more comprehensive explanation. To find the crux of this explanation, we have to investigate the resolution of substantive conflicts.

[39] Harry Eckstein, *A Theory of Stable Democracy*, Research Monograph No. 10 (Princeton: Center for International Studies, Princeton University, 1961), p. 11.

[40] Gabriel A. Almond and Sidney Verba, *The Civic Culture: Political Attitudes and Democracy in Five Nations* (Princeton: Princeton University Press, 1963), p. 21; see also chap. 12.

[41] See below, pp. 147–148, 154.

Chapter VI
THE SPIRIT OF ACCOMMODATION

Dutch politics is a politics of accommodation. That is the secret of its success. The term accommodation is here used in the sense of settlement of divisive issues and conflicts where only a minimal consensus exists. Pragmatic solutions are forged for all problems, even those with clear religious-ideological overtones on which the opposing parties may appear irreconcilable, and which therefore may seem insoluble and likely to split the country apart. A key element of this conception is the lack of a comprehensive political consensus, but not the complete absence of consensus. There must be a *minimum* of agreement on fundamentals. Dutch national consensus is weak and narrow, but it does contain the crucial component of a widely shared attitude that the existing system ought to be maintained and not be allowed to disintegrate. The second key requirement is

that the *leaders* of the self-contained blocs must be particularly convinced of the desirability of preserving the system.
And they must be willing and capable of bridging the gaps
between the mutually isolated blocs and of resolving serious
disputes in a largely nonconsensual context.

The politics of accommodation resembles politics at the
international level. In both, consensus is neither strong nor
extensive and all issues have to be negotiated by "national"
leaders. Sidney Verba expresses this parallel in characteriz-
ing a nonpluralist system:

> One can conceive of a political system made up of two closed
> camps with no overlapping of membership. The only channels
> of communication between the two camps would be at the
> highest level—say when the leaders of the two camps meet in
> the governing chambers—and all conflict would have to be
> resolved at this highest level. Politics comes to resemble
> negotiations between rival states; and war or a breakdown of
> negotiations is always possible.[1]

In Holland, accommodation has not broken down. War is
continually being averted, and the statesmen of the rival
blocs have managed to achieve peaceful coexistence.

THE ESTABLISHMENT OF THE
ACCOMMODATION PATTERN

The basic pattern of accommodation was
established in the period from 1878 to 1917 when the blocs
were pitted against each other on three divisive issues: the
question of church and state particularly with regard to education, the franchise issue, and the question of collective bargaining and the rights of labor. The modern political parties
were formed during this period with these three issues serving as catalysts.

[1] Sidney Verba, "Organizational Membership and Democratic
Consensus," *Journal of Politics*, Vol. 27, No. 3 (August 1965), p.
470.

The year 1878 marked the beginning of the open struggle over state aid to private schools, but the issue had its origins much earlier. The education act of 1806 established a virtual monopoly of religiously neutral public schools. Private schools could be set up only by special permission which was not granted frequently. This restriction was removed in 1857; private schools could now be founded freely but without financial support from the state. The Calvinists, led by G. Groen van Prinsterer, were far from satisfied. Groen van Prinsterer himself resigned from the Second Chamber but continued the fight outside of parliament.

Most Catholics, allied to the Liberals, supported the 1857 law. One Catholic representative in the First Chamber, Jonkheer C. E. J. T. van Nispen van Pannerden, defended the religiously neutral public school in almost purely Liberal terms: "If one would teach our youth from early childhood on that they must attend school only with other children of the same faith, one would already instill in their youthful hearts an aversion to those who follow a different religious conviction, and tolerance would thus certainly not be promoted. . . . Separate schools must lead to further divisions between the religions, and therefore to less tolerance. This I consider harmful."[2] But Catholic opinion would soon change, too. In 1864 Pope Pius IX issued the *Syllabus of Errors* condemning liberalism. Less than four years later, the Dutch bishops applied the papal dictates to the controversy over public and private schools in Holland. Their pastoral letter rejected all schools that were not exclusively Catholic: "The Church wants children to be instructed in the sciences, but also wants this instruction to be Catholic and religious in all respects."[3] The distance between the formerly allied Liberals

[2] Quoted in P. J. Oud, *Honderd jaren, 1840–1940: Een eeuw van staatkundige vormgeving in Nederland* (Assen: Van Gorcum, 1954), p. 63.

[3] Quoted in J. J. de Jong, *Politieke organisatie in West Europa na 1800* (The Hague: Nijhoff, 1951), p. 280.

and Catholics became even greater when a Liberal government recognized the conquest of the Papal State and with-
drew Dutch diplomatic representation from the Vatican in
1872.

At the same time, Calvinists and Catholics were discover-
ing their common objectives in education. At first, Groen
van Prinsterer had been opposed to the religiously neutral
public schools and had advocated public schools with a protestant character. This was, of course, not acceptable to the
Catholics. After his resignation from parliament he began
a crusade for a different alternative: private denominational
schools with full financial support from the state. On this
objective Catholics and Calvinists could agree without diffi-
culty. The line between these two religious blocs and the
Liberals became sharply drawn in 1878, when a Liberal government introduced a new education bill which kept the old
rule in force: not one penny of public aid to private schools.
Prime Minister J. Kappeyne van de Coppello defended the
proposal in a speech remarkable for its ideological character
and its implicit emphasis on the wide gulf between the religious and secular forces:

> What is our doctrine concerning the schools? We do not
> prevent you from establishing your own religious schools
> financed by your own resources. We do not compel your par-
> ents to send their children to our public schools. . . . But
> we cannot take the further step of making the secular author-
> ity subservient to the extension of your ecclesiastical power
> and of placing the money paid by the Dutch taxpayers at
> your disposal.[4]

A large-scale popular protest against the bill was organized
by the Calvinists. Out of this movement the Anti-Revolutionary party was born.

The law remained unchanged until 1889. Then, for the
first time, a limited degree of public support for private

[4] Quoted in Oud, *Honderd jaren*, p. 122.

schools was introduced. But the contribution amounted to less than a third of the costs of running the private schools, and no state aid was available for the establishment of new private schools. In 1904 and 1908 limited public aid was also extended to private secondary schools and universities, but Catholics and Calvinists demanded more. Emotions ran high, and in their joint election manifesto of 1913, the three Liberal parties accused the religious parties of organizing a reaction against "the principles of freedom and justice" and of "sharpening religious differences and extending them to all spheres of social life."[5] The issue of school aid remained basically unresolved while the cleavages between the contending groups became sharper and tensions increased.

The second divisive issue in the decades around the turn of the century was the question of extending the franchise. Direct elections to the Second Chamber were adopted in the constitutional amendments of 1848, but on an extremely restricted franchise. Only the well-to-do had the right to vote. This provision was not changed until 1887. Before the change, in 1880, only 12.3 per cent of adult males could vote. The two extensions of the franchise in 1887 and 1896 increased the size of the electorate to 26.8 per cent of adult males in 1890 and 49 per cent in 1900. Ten years later, more people had moved into the eligible categories, though no change was made in the electoral law, and the percentage increased to 63.2.[6]

From about 1880 on, the suffrage question was a major and divisive issue in Dutch politics. It caused a three-way split in the Liberal movement and the secession of conservative elements from the Anti-Revolutionary party who later founded the Christian Historical Union. At the beginning of the second decade of the twentieth century, demands for uni-

[5] Quoted *ibid*, p. 231.
[6] Centraal Bureau voor de Statistiek, *Statistiek der verkiezingen 1963: Tweede Kamer der Staten-Generaal, 15 mei* (Zeist: De Haan, 1963), p. 8.

versal suffrage became extremely insistent. More than a third of the adult male population were still barred from voting, and because women were not admitted to the franchise, more than two-thirds of the total adult population were disenfranchised. And no change in the electoral law had been made in almost fifteen years. Feelings on the issue were intense on both sides at the same time that emotions on the schools question reached a new height.

The third issue in the forty-year period from 1878 to 1917 was not as serious as the issues of the right to vote and public aid to private schools. The development of large-scale industries did not begin until about 1870, and before that there was little labor unrest. Strikes were virtually unknown; the English word "strike" was not replaced in Dutch parlance by the indigenous term *staking* until the 1870's. Labor's rights to organize and bargain collectively were never seriously challenged. The 1848 constitution guaranteed the freedom of association and assembly. The government could, according to the specific law on this subject enacted in 1855, intervene if organizations acted contrary to public law and order, but this was never used as a pretense for suppressing labor unions. Even after 1848 there was a law prohibiting strikes, but the government resorted to this law only four times, and it was abolished in 1872. Karl Marx, speaking in Amsterdam in that year, had good reasons to be favorably impressed: "There are countries like America, England, and, if I knew your institutions better, I would perhaps add Holland, where the workers can reach their goal by peaceful means."[7]

Partly as a result of the benevolent attitude of the government, the many labor unions that were set up from about 1870 on, tended to be moderate in their demands and actions. A Dutch section of the First International was estab-

[7] Quoted in I. J. Brugmans, *De arbeidende klasse in Nederland in de 19e eeuw (1813–1870)* (6th ed., Utrecht: Aula Boeken, 1963), p. 278. See also *ibid.*, pp. 186, 249–252, 273–278.

lished in Amsterdam in 1869, followed soon by sections in The Hague and Utrecht, but this movement was not very successful. A different militant union, the National Labor Secretariat founded in 1893, did develop considerable strength, but its power dissipated rapidly after the railroad strike of 1903. As a rival to this increasingly syndicalist and semi-anarchist union, a more moderate Socialist union (N.V.V.) was established in 1906. In 1894, the radical National Labor Secretariat was still the only national union and had a membership of 16,000. By 1910, however, its membership had declined to about 3,000, whereas the moderate N.V.V. had grown to a membership of no less than 41,000. In the same year, the moderate Catholic and Protestant unions had also passed the membership of the radical Secretariat: they had 12,000 and 7,000 members respectively. The relative moderation of the labor movement did not prevent the growth of severe strains in the relations between employers and workers, especially in the years around 1910. Hoefnagels points out that it is symptomatic that employers frequently used the weapon of the lockout. From 1904 to 1917, the number of labor days lost in lockouts equaled more than half the number of days lost in strikes. And in some years lockouts were even more common. In 1910, for instance, the time lost in lockouts was nearly three times greater than the time lost in strikes.[8]

Around 1910, therefore, the political situation looked quite serious. The three major issues had reached a peak of tension, and the lines between the rivals were sharply drawn. Especially the issues of the schools and the right to vote remained fundamentally unresolved with all of the contending groups hardening in their intention not to yield. The cabinet that took office in 1913 recognized the danger of allowing

[8] H. Hoefnagels, *Een eeuw sociale problematiek: Van sociaal conflict naar strategische samenwerking* (Assen: Van Gorcum, 1957), pp. 114, 122.

the conflicts to continue, and courageously decided to attempt a solution to the dilemma. Prime Minister P. W. A. Cort van der Linden described the role of his cabinet as that of an "honest broker" between the rivals, and expressed his opinion on the schools controversy as follows:

> The political battle over the schools issue is a wedge, so to speak, driven into our national life and splitting our nation into two nations. Not only the right but also the left are keenly aware of the fact that our nation cannot develop vigorously and cannot release the energy which we must have at our disposal, unless this wedge is removed from our national life. The government is of the opinion that they would be able to perform a beneficial service to the nation, if they would be successful in finding a basis for ending this unfortunate impediment to our national development.[9]

The government appealed to the contending parties to accommodate their differences, and to put the necessity of achieving a solution ahead of ideological principles and antagonisms. The parties reacted favorably. In December 1913 a special commission was formed to attempt a solution for the schools question. All seven political parties—Catholics, Anti-Revolutionaries, the Christian Historical Union, Social Democrats, and the three Liberal parties—were represented on the fourteen-member commission, each party sending its leader and its principal education expert. A similar commission to consider the franchise problem had been set up a month earlier. The latter commission submitted its recommendations in 1914; the former was ready in March 1916.

The recommendations of the commissions were adopted virtually without change. All elementary schools, public and private, were to get the same financial assistance from the government in proportion to their enrollments. Universal manhood suffrage would be adopted based on the list system of proportional representation. The proposals embody-

[9] Quoted in Oud, *Honderd jaren*, p. 237.

ing these solutions were passed by parliament with only one or two votes against and sometimes with complete unanimity. The debates took place in 1916 and 1917, during the First World War. This international emergency enhanced the sense of urgency behind the near-unanimity, but it was not the decisive factor. The process of accommodation was started in 1913, before the outbreak of the war. The enactment of the solutions required constitutional amendments which had to be approved by two successive parliaments in order to enter into force. So anxious were the parties not to endanger the settlement that they turned the required election between the first and second readings of the constitutional amendments—designed to let the people have a voice in changing the constitution—into a formality. They entered into an agreement allowing all incumbents to win re-election. The plan worked and the new parliament, an exact replica of the old one, gave its final stamp of approval in 1917.[10]

This crucial episode set the pattern of the politics of accommodation. Three special characteristics of the pattern deserve emphasis: (1) the pre-eminent role of the top leaders in recognizing the problems and in realistically finding solutions in spite of ideological disagreements—a process in which the rank and file were largely ignored even to the extent of rigging an important election; (2) the participation of the leaders of *all* blocs in the settlement; and (3) the importance of the principle of proportionality in the substance of the settlement—state aid to education on the basis of proportional treatment of all schools and representation in future parliaments on the basis of the proportion of the vote received by each party. This set of solutions is referred to in Holland as the *Pacificatie*, which may be translated as "peaceful settlement," a term usually applied to international

---

[10] *Ibid.*, pp. 231–248. C. W. de Vries, *Schets eener parlementaire geschiedenis van Nederland: 1914–1918* (4th ed., The Hague: Nijhoff, 1955), Vol. 4, pp. 142–183. Women received the right to vote in 1919.

politics but also appropriate to the politics of accommodation.

The politics of accommodation is based on a high degree of self-containment and mutual isolation of the four blocs with overarching contact among the blocs limited to the elite level. The success of this system depends to a large extent on the leaders' joint efforts at peace-keeping and peaceful change. The Roman Catholic bishops tersely described this pattern of high-level cooperation among the blocs and affirmed their favorable judgment of it in their 1954 pastoral letter, with the characteristic provisos that it should be restricted to "leading persons, well-trained within our own sphere" and that all Catholics should remain "unified and strong" as a separate bloc.[11]

Since the establishment of the basic pattern of the politics of accommodation in 1917, the process of negotiation among the bloc leaders has become more institutionalized. It takes place, in the words of the Dutch Reformed Synod, within "so-called summit organizations."[12] From informal and ad hoc contacts, it has moved to formal and more or less permanent institutions, and finally to official organizations anchored in the country's legal-constitutional framework. Or, in the terminology of international politics with which the politics of accommodation has been compared earlier, traditional diplomacy has increasingly been replaced by international organization diplomacy with its permanent institutional framework, and by some degree of confederal cooperation. This does not mean that ad hoc summit diplomacy

[11] Bisschoppelijk mandement, *De Katholiek in het openbare leven van deze tijd* (Utrecht: 1954), p. 13.

[12] Generale Synode van de Nederlandse Hervormde Kerk, *Christen-zijn in de Nederlandse samenleving* (The Hague:: Boekencentrum, 1955), p. 5. See also above, pp. 93–94.

has been abandoned; it still plays a major role in the settlement of sudden and unusual crises. But for the accommodation of the usual and predictable problems and conflicts, the elite can resort to permanently established confederal organs.

The crown on this intricate system is the Social and Economic Council. It consists of 45 members: 15 representative of the labor unions, 15 representative of the employers, and 15 members appointed by the cabinet. The labor-union representatives are chosen by the large Socialist, Catholic, and Protestant unions in proportion to their total memberships (7:5:3). The employers' representatives are mainly chosen by the large employers, farmers, and retailers associations of the Liberal, Catholic, and Calvinist blocs. The members chosen by the cabinet are individual experts, primarily professors of law or economics, but these positions are also carefully apportioned among the blocs. The law stipulates that all members vote independently and cannot be bound by the organizations they represent. In practice, this provision makes little difference because the representatives are usually the top leaders of their organizations. The Council is, therefore, a permanent confederal organ in which the leaders of all organizationally separate interest groups that are important in the economic realm, meet and compromise.

The Council's formal powers are limited. It heads the comprehensive statutory organization to be established in all branches of industry, but the execution of this plan is still in its infancy. It can also make rules, with the force of law, for industry, but only with two-thirds majorities and subject to cabinet veto. The Council's advisory power, however, gives it its political importance. The cabinet is required by law to seek the Council's advice on all proposed social and economic measures, unless this should be contrary to the national interest. The Council can also volunteer advice to the government. This advice is often tantamount to future national policy. Especially when the Council is united, both cabinet and parliament are presented with a *fait accompli,* because the "advice" represents the accommodation achieved by the leaders of the most powerful interest groups. The political significance of the Council is also enhanced by its frequent practice, permitted by law, to deliberate in secret and to keep the resulting advice to the cabinet secret. One can say without exaggeration that the Council ranks in the same category of political power and significance as the cabinet and parliament. In this respect, it presents a sharp contrast to the weakness of economic parliaments elsewhere.[13]

The Council, with its formal status in the constitutional framework, its comprehensive task, and its permanent staff, represents the pinnacle of the institutionalization of the accommodation process. It was established in 1950, as the end product of a slow incremental process starting shortly after 1917. During the interwar period, high-level informal contacts both among the employers organizations and among the labor unions became more frequent. Moreover, opportunities for meeting between these two groups—employers and workers—were presented in a number of advisory bodies set up by the cabinet, especially the High Council of Labor with a tripartite composition similar to the present Social and Economic Council. In 1928, the chairmen of the employers associations and the chairmen of the labor unions decided to get together for more or less regular consultations. At first, these meetings were informal but a permanent consultative committee was set up in 1938. During the years of German occupation in the Second World War, plans were made secretly to formalize and expand the high-level con-

[13] For short descriptions of the Social and Economic Council, see Georg Geismann, *Politische Struktur und Regierungssytem in den Niederlanden*, Kölner Schriften zur Politischen Wissenschaft, Vol. 4 (Frankfurt am Main and Bonn: Athenäum Verlag, 1964), pp. 116–118; Alan D. Robinson, *Dutch Organised Agriculture in International Politics* (The Hague: Nijhoff, 1961), pp. 50–52; and J. E. Andriessen, S. Miedema, and C. J. Oort, *De sociaal-economische besturing van Nederland* (3rd ed., Groningen: Noordhoff, 1966), pp. 105–123.

tacts between the leaders of labor and industry. The Foundation of Labor was established in 1945, and it in turn paved the way for the establishment of the Social and Economic Council five years later.[14]

A similar development took place in agriculture. From 1922 on, the leaders of the three farmers associations held annual meetings. During the depression years, the farm workers unions were also frequently included in some of the deliberations. Shortly before the outbreak of the war in 1940, lengthy discussions took place and a permanent organ of consultation was set up the following year: the Central Secretariat for Agriculture and Horticulture. Because of the intervention of the German occupation authorities, its work ceased soon, but secret contacts continued. In 1945 the Foundation of Agriculture, paralleling the Foundation of Labor, was established. The final step toward full institutionalization was taken in 1954 when the Foundation was replaced by the Board of Agriculture (*Landbouwschap*) operating under the Social and Economic Council.[15]

ACCOMMODATION AFTER 1917

The settlement of 1917 established the basic pattern for the resolution of future conflicts, and at the same time solved two deeply vexing problems. Of course, it did not affect the social structure in the sense of integrating

[14] D. U. Stikker, "1940–1945: De wording van de Stichting van den Arbeid," in P. J. Bouman, et al., eds., *150 Jaar Koninkrijk der Nederlanden* (Amsterdam: De Bussy, 1963), pp. 248–257. See also John P. Windmuller, "Postwar Wage Determination in the Netherlands," *Annals of the American Academy of Political and Social Science*, Vol. 310 (March 1957), pp. 109–122.

[15] Robinson, pp. 55–57. There are also a number of less important official advisory bodies (like the Social Insurance Council set up in 1952) and unofficial organs of consultation (like the confederal associations formed by the separate radio and television organizations and by the press). See M. Rooij, "Is de Nederlandse pers verzuild?" in P. H. van Gorkum, ed., *Pacificatie en de zuilen* (Meppel: J. A. Boom, 1965), p. 59.

the rival blocs, and other religious and class issues were bound to arise. In fact, the settlement helped the blocs to become more firmly entrenched within their own spheres by giving them secure and exclusive control over their parties and schools.

Religious issues continued to require accommodation *between* the blocs. On some issues the Calvinist forces have clashed with the Catholics; on others the combined religious forces have been pitted against the secular bloc. But because of the religious homogeneity of the blocs, religious questions have not been inducive to create tensions *within* their ranks (except between the Reformed and Dutch Reformed denominations in the Calvinist bloc). Class issues, on the other hand, have been issues both *between* and *within* the blocs. The Socialist and Liberal blocs are divided from each other by class differences, but the Catholic and Calvinist blocs have a heterogeneous class composition. Class issues, therefore, have to be resolved within the religious blocs, and this has given their parties a crucial role in politics.

Since 1917 religious questions have continued to plague Dutch politics but they have rarely been sufficiently divisive to threaten the stability of the system. The only major exceptions were the controversies over diplomatic relations with the Vatican and Princess Irene's conversion to Catholicism in 1964. Holland's diplomatic post at the Vatican had been abolished in 1872, but was restored during the First World War for international diplomatic reasons, and continued in existence after the war. This was welcomed by the Catholics but a thorn in the flesh of the Calvinists, especially the Christian Historical Union. In 1925 the Second Chamber struck the funds for the Vatican post from the budget of the Ministry of Foreign Affairs, provoking a cabinet crisis and severely straining Catholic-Calvinist relations. During the Second World War, diplomatic relations were restored, again because of the wartime importance of the Vatican as a diplomatic center. The decision entailed a subtle but important change: this time, the new Dutch envoy at the Vatican was to be a Protestant rather than a Catholic like his two predecessors from 1915 to 1925. A new attack on the Vatican post in the Second Chamber was beaten back by 65 to 9 votes in 1946—the 9 votes cast primarily by members of the Christian Historical Union. The issue gradually lost its emotional overtones thereafter. In 1956 the cabinet was even able to appoint a Catholic. When Labor party leader J. A. W. Burger complained that the cabinet had changed its policy on this matter without consulting the Second Chamber, Foreign Minister J. W. Beyen answered that the ambassador's religion should be irrelevant—which indeed it was in the changed atmosphere of the 1950's. The controversy was successfully accommodated when it was still a sensitive question, and subsequently disappeared altogether as a political issue.[16]

Irene's conversion, which posed a more serious problem because it threatened to undermine the fragile national consensus, was also successfully accommodated.[17] Other representative religious issues include the banning of religious processions in the North of the country—which is also a typical compromise: processions are allowed in the Catholic South but not in the mainly Protestant North—the appointment of humanist "chaplains" in the armed forces, strict observance of Sunday as a religious holiday, and the laws governing cremation and gambling. On such issues the blocs have widely divergent opinions. For instance, a 1965 opinion poll found that 64 per cent of the Liberals were in favor of legalizing roulette in seaside resorts and only 11 per cent were opposed. Of the supporters of the Protestant parties,

[16] Letters to the author by parliamentary expert P. J. Oud (dated June 20, 1966) and W. H. Vermeulen of the University of Utrecht (dated June 28, 1966). See also P. J. Oud, *Het jongste verleden: Parlementaire geschiedenis van Nederland 1918–1940*, 6 vols. (Assen: Van Gorcum, 1948–51), Vol. 3, pp. 62–81.

[17] See also above, pp. 84–86, and below, pp. 129–130.

only 8 per cent favored the idea and 74 per cent opposed
it.[18] But although these are sensitive questions they are not
issues of major importance. It is important to realize that in
almost all countries where religion is a divisive factor, the
crucial issue concerns the relationship between the state and
private denominational schools. Once this question is resolved, religious cleavages lose much of their political salience. The relative peace among the religious blocs in Holland after 1917 must be attributed, to a large extent, to the
pacific settlement of the schools controversy. Other religious
differences have not disappeared, but they are only minor
irritants.

The main politically significant issues after 1917 have
been social and economic. The franchise problem was settled in 1917, but other big problems remained, especially
those concerning the ways of fighting the depression of the
1930's and the creation of the welfare state. Vitally important elements in the successful handling of these issues have
been not only the Social and Economic Council and its predecessors, but also the mitigation of tensions on these questions by the heterogeneous class composition of the Catholic
and Calvinist blocs. These blocs and their political and social
organizations are, like the Socialist and Liberal blocs, religiously homogeneous, but, unlike the Socialists and Liberals, cut across class lines. On issues affecting class interests,
the Catholics and Calvinists are not automatically united
within their own ranks. Compromises must be reached first
within these blocs. As a result, the religious parties usually
take a middle-of-the-road position, and this, in turn, has a
moderating effect on the entire political system.

The role of the Catholic party is especially important in
this respect. It has become the axis around which Dutch
political life revolves. The Protestant parties are also center

[18] Nederlands Instituut voor de Publieke Opinie, *Bericht No.
1034* (January 27, 1965).

parties, but they are divided into Anti-Revolutionaries and the Christian Historical Union (plus usually a number of fundamentalist Calvinist splinter parties), and their combined electoral strength is far less than that of the Catholic party. Furthermore, one of the Protestant parties—the Christian Historical Union—has very weak party discipline, and can contribute some strength but no great reliability to the political center. In contrast, the Catholic party has always shown great strength and disciplined unity. In the years before the introduction of proportional representation in 1917, the Catholics usually held close to one-fourth of the seats in the Second Chamber; after 1917 they comprised close to one-third of the Chamber. Since 1901, they have been the largest single group in the Chamber with only one exception: from 1956 to 1959, the Labor party held one more seat.

The center position and the parliamentary strength of the Catholic party have made it an indispensable partner in cabinet coalitions. In the three major alliances which characterize Dutch political history after 1848, the Catholic party has always been one of the partners: in the Liberal-Catholic alliance predominant from 1848 to 1878, the Calvinist-Catholic alliance predominant from 1888 to 1925, and the Labor-Catholic alliance after the Second World War. These alliances did not rule without interruption, but they were the usual governing coalitions during each of the periods. Since 1918, the Catholic party has participated in all cabinets with only two minor exceptions: a cabinet in 1939 which was voted out of office only three days after it had been formed, and, for a relatively brief time, the government-in-exile in London which was not under parliamentary control.[19]

[19] H. Daalder, "Parties and Politics in the Netherlands," *Political Studies*, Vol. 3, No. 1 (February 1955), p. 7; Robert C. Bone, "The Dynamics of Dutch Politics," *Journal of Politics*, Vol. 24, No. 1 (February 1962), pp. 31–33. See also W. A. M. van Eekeren, "The Catholic People's Party in the Netherlands" (unpublished doctoral dissertation, Georgetown University, 1956).

TABLE 21. OPINION OF PARTY SUPPORTERS ON
CABINET COALITIONS
(In per cent)

| Supporters of party | New cabinet should be formed by | | | | |
	Catholic party	Labor party	Liberal party	Anti-Rev. party	Chr. Hist. Union
Catholic	83	31	21	19	17
Labor	53	65	15	14	20
Liberal	59	21	65	41	38
Anti-Revo-lutionary	50	11	26	66	53
Chr. Hist. Union	57	19	36	50	67

SOURCE: Nederlands Instituut voor de publieke Opinie, *Bericht No. 946* (May 30, 1963).

The paramount position of the Catholic party is not only taken for granted by the leaders of the other parties in the negotiations preceding the formation of new cabinets, but is also widely accepted by the rank and file of the non-Catholic parties. Shortly after the parliamentary elections of 1963, the Netherlands Institute of Public Opinion included the following question in a sample survey: "In your opinion, which party or parties should form a new government?" The Catholic party was named by 57 per cent of the respondents, a much higher percentage than for any of the other parties; the Labor party was mentioned by only 35 per cent, the Christian Historical Union by 26 per cent, the Anti-Revolutionaries by 25 per cent, and the Liberals by 23 per cent. These results are even more interesting when they are crosstabulated by the party preference of the respondents (see Table 21). As expected, the strongest preference of each group of voters is for their own party to enter the new cabinet, and many supporters of the two Protestant parties also indicate that they favor a place for the other Protestant party in the cabinet. It is significant that the next highest percentage among the supporters of all other parties is for the Catholic party.

The Catholic party thus makes a major contribution to the stability of Dutch democracy. It is the governing party par excellence.

Chapter VII
THE RULES OF THE GAME

The politics of accommodation places heavy burdens on the political leaders. Successful policymaking and settlement of divisive issues under the adverse conditions of a minimally consensual milieu requires a clear recognition of the perennial disintegrative tendencies in the system and the capability to take either preventive or remedial action. In the Netherlands, the process of accommodation is greatly facilitated by the existence of a number of rules that govern the "game" of accommodation. These rules are not part of a comprehensive national consensus; they apply mainly to the political elite. Or, to follow the terminology of political culture analysis, the rules of the game are a part of the "role culture" developed by and instilled in the elite, and not of the mass culture.[1] Furthermore, they consist of a mixture of procedural rules and general orientations

[1] See Gabriel A. Almond and Sidney Verba, *The Civic Culture: Political Attitudes and Democracy in Five Nations* (Princeton: Princeton University Press, 1963), pp. 29–31. These rules of the game differ in the same way from what Truman calls the "rules of the

toward politics, and do not have much substantive content. It must be emphasized that the seven rules specified below are unwritten, informal, and implicit. No convenient book of rules exists; they have to be inferred from the actions of the leaders especially under conditions of political tension.[2]

RULE I: THE BUSINESS OF POLITICS

The first and foremost rule of the Dutch political game is that politics should not be regarded as a game at all. It is, to borrow von Clausewitz's phrase, "a serious means to a serious end." Or, to put it even more succinctly, it is a business. This attitude is in accord with Holland's long tradition as a merchant nation and with the crucial political role the merchant middle classes have played in Dutch history. This attitude toward politics has a pervasive and highly beneficial influence on democratic stability. Hans Daalder calls it the "businesslike determination that the job should not be allowed to suffer"; and Alan D. Robinson refers to the "attitude that doctrinal disputes should not stand in the way of getting the work done."[3] The political elite is oriented toward results. In this respect, Dutch politics is sharply different from what Nathan Leites has called the "game of politics in France" with its tactics of delay, equivocation, and avoidance of responsibility, regardless of the consequences for the nation.[4]

---

game" (i.e. the "general ideological consensus"); see above, pp. 13–14.

[2] Hans Daalder has done the most significant pioneering work in calling attention to these rules. See especially his *Leiding en lijdelijkheid in de Nederlandse politiek* (Assen: Van Gorcum, 1964).

[3] H. Daalder, "Parties and Politics in the Netherlands," *Political Studies*, Vol. 3, No. 1 (February 1955), p. 16; Alan D. Robinson, *Dutch Organised Agriculture in International Politics* (The Hague, Nijhoff, 1961), p. 37. See also Daalder, "Politiek in Nederlands kader," in *Mensen en machten* (Utrecht: Spectrum, 1965), pp. 117–118.

[4] Nathan Leites, *On the Game of Politics in France* (Stanford: Stanford University Press, 1959), passim.

Without this result-oriented attitude, Dutch politics would look quite different. Neither the great political settlement of 1917 nor the continuing pattern of accommodation since then would have been possible without it. It is the axiom underlying all other "rules of the political business."

RULE II: THE AGREEMENT TO DISAGREE

Probably the second most important rule that governs the Dutch political business is the pragmatic acceptance of the ideological differences as basic realities which cannot and should not be changed. The fundamental convictions of other blocs must be tolerated, if not respected. Disagreements must not be allowed to turn into either mutual contempt or proselytizing zeal.

In the policy-making process, a pure and consistent application of this rule would lead to paralysis. Decisions on controversial matters have to be made, and continuous inaction would have disastrous consequences. In its pure form, therefore, the rule is only applied to questions not requiring immediate answers. An excellent illustration is the cabinet crisis of 1951. The four-party coalition cabinet, based on all major parties except the Anti-Revolutionaries, fell apart on the highly emotional issue of colonial policy. In the negotiations to end the crisis, it was clear that the realities of both the international situation and the domestic constellation of opinion would not permit any major change of policy. The four parties were thus able to mend their differences by simply agreeing to disagree on the colonial question because it had no direct policy consequences. The new cabinet was a virtual carbon copy of its predecessor, and could be formed only because of the conviction that the widely divergent and deeply felt disagreements over colonial policy should not stand in the way of fruitful cooperation on more pressing questions. This policy, or rather nonpolicy, was appropriately referred to as the "icebox policy."[5] Here the agreement to disagree allowed a vexatious issue to be temporarily frozen.

Such perfect conditions for the pure and simple application of the agreement-to-disagree rule are rare, of course. Most issues do require some kind of substantive decision. An attempt is then made to involve all blocs in finding a fair compromise. Or, if a compromise acceptable to all blocs cannot be reached because of ideological opposition by one or more blocs, the other groups will go to great lengths in trying to avoid antagonizing their opponents. Decisions are not made by a majority simply outvoting a minority. For instance, when a cabinet proposal to institute a football pool was debated in parliament in 1960 and again in 1964, the Calvinists, and especially the orthodox Anti-Revolutionary party, were fundamentally opposed on religious grounds— not allowing any pragmatic compromise. On the other hand, a large majority were in favor and had the votes to pass the bill over Calvinist opposition. But this was not done. The majority parties made a number of concessions—like limiting the amount an individual could wager and instituting a relatively low maximum for the highest prize to be won—not so much in order to fashion a majority to pass the bill, but mainly to placate the minority. This also made it possible for the Anti-Revolutionaries to remain in the cabinet.

In this form, the agreement-to-disagree rule comes close to Calhoun's doctrine of concurrent majority. On issues considered vital by any bloc, no decision can be made without either their concurrence or at least substantial concessions to them. The veto power is not absolute. No single group can block action completely, but its wishes will be considered seriously and accommodated as much as possible by the others. In short, the rule is majoritarianism tempered by the spirit of concurrent majority.

[5] See Arend Lijphart, *The Trauma of Decolonization: The Dutch and West New Guinea* (New Haven: Yale University Press, 1966), pp. 164–177.

RULE III: SUMMIT DIPLOMACY

The politics of accommodation entails government by the elite. The leaders of the religious-ideological blocs have the duty to make the political decisions and to work out compromises. This pattern has become increasingly more institutionalized, as was discussed in the previous chapter.[6]

The more serious the political question that is at stake, the higher will be the elite level at which it will be resolved. This means that the crucial issues have to be handled at the summit. The problems of state aid to religious schools and of extending the suffrage were solved by summit conferences of the top leaders of all major parties. This culminated in the peaceful settlement of 1917.[7] Summit diplomacy was resorted to again in later crises. When the Germans occupied Holland in May 1940, the cabinet went into exile and parliament disbanded. But the political leaders remaining in the Netherlands decided immediately on the necessity of close cooperation. An informal summit conference was established which consisted of twelve persons: the two highest leaders of each of the six major parties (Catholics, Social Democrats, Anti-Revolutionaries, Christian Historical Union, and the two Liberal parties in existence at that time). This important group, which eventually received the unpretentious name of "Political Council" (*Politiek Convent*), met for the first time on July 1, 1940, and continued to be active in one form or another during the entire war period in spite of growing Nazi persecution.[8]

Another example was the group referred to in popular

[6] See above, pp. 112–115.
[7] See above, pp. 109–112.
[8] W. Drees, "1940–1945: Het Politiek Convent," in P. J. Bouman, et al., eds., *150 Jaar Koninkrijk der Nederlanden* (Amsterdam: De Bussy, 1963), pp. 232–239. See also Werner Warmbrunn, *The Dutch under German Occupation: 1940–1945* (Stanford: Stanford University Press, 1963), pp. 216–218.

parlance as the "Irene Quartet." Its task was to resolve the crisis over Princess Irene's conversion and marriage in 1964. It consisted of four cabinet ministers: Prime Minister V. G. M. Marijnen, his second-in-command B. W. Biesheuvel, Minister of Internal Affairs E. H. Toxopeus, and Minister of Justice Y. Scholten. These four were chosen ostensibly on the grounds that the issue involved their special jurisdictions as ministers. But it was no accident that they also belonged to the four different parties represented in the cabinet. The only gap in this summit arrangement was the absence of a Labor party leader from the temporary supercabinet. A Laborite was not included because the party was in the opposition from 1958 to 1965, but the Irene Quartet was informally in close touch with the Labor party leadership, too.

A somewhat similar arrangement is the so-called "Seniors' Assembly" (*Seniorenconvent*) in the Second Chamber of the States-General. It is a five-man committee made up of the parliamentary chairmen of the five major parties. It has no formal status, and it operates only intermittently.[9] But it assumes great political significance at times of actual or threatening crises and deadlocks in the chamber.

RULE IV: PROPORTIONALITY

The rule of proportionality is a simple procedural device capable of solving a host of troublesome problems. The most important of these is the allocation of the necessarily scarce financial resources at the government's disposal. The peaceful settlement of the schools issue in 1917 set the pattern: all schools, private as well as public, would receive government funds in proportion to the number of students enrolled. The same rule is applied in the allocation of governmental assistance to hospitals and other welfare functions. It does not solve the problem of deciding the *kinds* of

[9] E. van Raalte, *Het Nederlandse Parlement* (The Hague: Staatsdrukkerij- en Uitgeverijbedrijf, 1958), p. 155.

projects the government should finance; for example, should more money be spent on secondary education or on hospital expansion or on land reclamation? But once this decision is made, it does solve the problem of allocation among the blocs, which is politically the most sensitive one. Hans Daalder puts it this way: "the essence of political action has shifted from strife to distribution" with the government's task limited to "the allocation of subsidies according to objective criteria."[10]

Proportionality applies to other areas as well. Network time on the state-owned radio and television stations is allocated to the bloc organizations that arrange virtually all programs, roughly in proportion to their memberships. Appointments to public office are on the basis of a rough proportionality. The almost one thousand burgomasters and the eleven provincial governors are appointed with the idea of approximate proportionality in mind. The composition of the national civil service in The Hague is patterned after the relative strengths of the blocs in the population as a whole, although the Catholics are still slightly underrepresented.[11] It is significant, however, that the Catholics invariably base their protests against this bias on the grounds of injustice defined as lack of proportionality. Such an argument is most persuasive and is bound to win eventually. In the local civil services, proportionality is also the rule. Gadourek reports the formula, based on both the number of civil servants belonging to each bloc and their salaries, used by the town council in the small town of Sassenheim:

> The total amount of money for the salaries of the personnel is divided among them roughly in the same way as the electorate

[10] Daalder, *Leiding en lijdelijkheid in the Nederlandse politiek*, p. 24. See also S. W. Couwenberg, "Nederland meer een corporatieve dan parlementaire democratie," *Oost-West*, Vol. 3., No. 7 (October 1964), p. 228.
[11] See above, pp. 90–92.

is divided into various political (virtually *religious*) factions. Thus, for instance, if about one half of the population is Roman Catholic, the money which is paid to the Roman Catholic clerks at the village-hall will amount to about one half of the total sum. Hirings are governed by the same rule. As there are no sudden changes in the political composition of the electorate, elections do not disturb this system.[12]

The rule of proportionality is of fundamental importance to the success of the politics of accommodation in Holland. The establishment of the accommodation pattern of politics by the peaceful settlement of 1917 was intimately related to this rule: both the suffrage and the schools questions were settled on the basis of proportionality. The rule has been faithfully adhered to ever since.

RULE V: DEPOLITICIZATION

Proportionality is one method for the neutralization of potentially divisive political disputes. But it can be applied only when there are valued items like appointments, subsidies, or broadcast hours to be distributed. A different method for neutralizing sensitive issues and justifying compromises to the rank and file, especially in postwar politics, has been the use of complicated economic arguments and the juggling of economic facts and figures incomprehensible to most people.

Another frequent tool of depoliticization is the resort to legal and constitutional principles. The handling of the crisis over Princess Irene's conversion and marriage can again serve as an example. The issue was most embarrassing: should a Catholic be allowed to ascend the Dutch throne? A positive answer would deeply offend especially the more

[12] I. Gadourek, *A Dutch Community: Social and Cultural Structure and Process in a Bulb-Growing Region in the Netherlands* (2nd ed., Groningen: Wolters, 1961), p. 62.

orthodox Calvinists, and a negative answer would be an insult to the Catholics. If the issue had been limited to Irene's conversion to Catholicism, the agreement-to-disagree rule could have been followed: the government could have argued that the constitution did not bar Catholics from succession to the throne, but that Irene was not first in the line of succession and that hence the issue was purely hypothetical. Thus the dilemma could perhaps have been avoided altogether, and at least postponed. But the question was more difficult: a definite decision on Irene's right of succession was absolutely necessary, because of the constitutional provision that royal marriages require parliamentary approval. Irene was engaged to a Spanish nobleman. Without parliamentary approval, she and her descendants would be excluded from the right of succession.

Coincidentally, Irene's fiancé was involved in Spanish politics. The possibility of a future prince consort being embroiled in politics, and even more seriously, in the politics of a foreign country, definitely conflicted with an important unwritten rule in the Dutch constitution: the monarch and the royal family must stay out of politics. This was the main argument on which the cabinet based its decision not to propose parliamentary consent to the marriage. Thus the most troublesome issue—which concerned the monarch's religion and which was therefore a potential strain on interbloc peaceful coexistence—could be avoided. If a decision on a Catholic princess' right to become the Dutch queen would have been inescapable, the government and parliament would undoubtedly have supported this right—the Catholic, Socialist, and Liberal leaders whole-heartedly, and the leaders of the two main Protestant parties perhaps more reluctantly. But such a decision was not necessary, because the issue could be formulated in less embarrassing and, therefore, politically more acceptable terms. It was deliberately neutralized by the skillful resort to a generally approved constitutional principle.

RULE VI: SECRECY

Successful accommodation by the bloc leaders requires a high degree of flexibility. They have to be able to make concessions and to arrive at pragmatic compromises even when religious or ideological values are at stake. The process of accommodation must, therefore, be shielded from publicity. The leaders' moves in negotiations among the blocs must be carefully insulated from the knowledge of the rank and file. Because an "information gap" is desirable, secrecy is a most important rule. In this respect, the politics of accommodation again resembles international politics. Woodrow Wilson's prescriptions of "open covenants of peace, openly arrived at" and a "diplomacy [which] shall proceed always frankly and in the public view"[13] are obstacles to compromise between ideologically opposed rivals in the international as well as in domestic systems. In Holland, covenants are usually, though not always, open, but covenants openly arrived at are rare indeed.

Democracy would suffocate under complete secrecy, of course. The principal public forum for the discussion and disclosure of political facts and issues is the States-General, and particularly the Second Chamber. Here the parties confront each other and the cabinet in the presence of the parliamentary reporters of the major newspapers and those citizens who are lucky enough to gain access to the two short rows of seats—a symbolically significant limitation!—of the public gallery.[14] Parliamentary approval represents no more than the final stage of the accommodation process. Until recently, all meetings of parliamentary committees were closed to the public. What is held up for public view on the floor of the chambers is the result of the interbloc negotiations which

[13] Albert Bushnell Hart, ed., *Selected Addresses and Public Papers of Woodrow Wilson* (New York: Boni and Liveright, 1918), p. 248.

[14] However, in recent years a number of important parliamentary debates have been televised.

now merely requires ratification. Covenants that were worked out in secret, now become open. Daalder characterizes parliamentary debates as "more elaborate than informative . . . because policy has already been determined in another place and because a compromise itself looks much better in half-lights than in the glare of a real parliamentary search-light."[15] Clashes between the chamber and the cabinet do occur, of course; amendments are introduced and often passed; and adverse votes can topple cabinets. But the leaders usually do their utmost to avoid it, and to safeguard at least the essence of the *fait accompli*. And when the parliamentary battle gets out of control, they often resort to the device of suspending the public debate and retiring to the proverbial "smoke-filled rooms."

Parliament does have considerable constitutional powers to force the cabinet into a public disclosure of facts: investigation, interpellation, and questions. The most potent of these—parliamentary investigation—has been used only nine times since 1850, and mainly before 1887. From 1887 to 1947, no commissions of investigation were set up. The best-known instance of investigation since the Second World War is the nine-member commission which labored for almost ten years on a thorough inquiry into the activities of the wartime government-in-exile in London—more a matter of historical interest than of current political excitement. Interpellations are held more frequently: in the 1930's about ten per year, but no more than four or five per year in the postwar period. This is, therefore, not a strong weapon against elite secrecy either. Besides, secrecy is safeguarded by the custom that the interpellator submits his questions in advance to the minister involved. The most innocuous parliamentary weapon is the question. Hundreds of questions are asked during each annual session, but the overwhelming

[15] H. Daalder, "The Relation Between Cabinet and Parliament in the Netherlands" (unpublished paper presented at the Rome Congress of the International Political Science Association, 1958), p. 17.

majority deal with very minor matters and are written. And ministers usually take their time to write the answers. Few questions entail a lively confrontation on the floor of the chambers.[16] In short, parliament has the power to bridge the information gap but does not take advantage of it. Its members, or at least those belonging to the Big Five of the parties, conscientiously participate in the conspiracy of silence.

The academic world also tends to protect this secrecy. Goudsblom, pointing out that the question of social stratification in Holland has not been subjected to a thorough scholarly investigation and that "least of all is known about the elites," speculates that one reason for this lack of information is the elite's "discretion [which] has always been part and parcel of its self-assured dignity and authority; the modern university graduates, ascended from lower levels of society, have generally tended without questioning to adopt this paternalistic attitude."[17]

There are other conspirators, too, notably the press. Indeed the communications elite play the most vital role in preserving the secrecy of the accommodation process. Most of the national newspapers are closely linked to a particular bloc by organizational, ideological, or personal ties. Editors and journalists belong to the "establishment" of the politics of accommodation. An independent paper like *De Telegraaf* is more adventurous and does not feel bound to guard all political secrets. But its access to such classified information is severely limited, and it tends to be more noisy than knowledgeable.

In a speech to the National Newspaper Association in 1964, Prime Minister Marijnen cautioned the press to exercise self-control in deciding what is and what is not fit to print[18]—a totally unnecessary reminder to the highly self-

[16] Van Raalte, pp. 207–217, 232–238.

[17] Johan Goudsblom, *Dutch Society* (New York: Random House, 1967), p. 70.

[18] *Nieuwe Rotterdamse Courant* (May 26, 1964).

disciplined Dutch newspaperman. In commenting on the editorial speculation of another paper, the *Nieuwe Rotterdamse Courant* wrote: "They give the impression of knowing more than they can tell at the moment (which is not abnormal for newspapers; they are often like icebergs)."[19] This would also be an apt description of the entire political process, of which only a small part is visible and the rest is kept hidden under the dark and sometimes muddy water.

RULE VII: THE GOVERNMENT'S RIGHT TO GOVERN

All rules discussed so far are closely related to the first rule or axiom that politics is a serious business. The seventh rule is a direct deduction from this axiom. What is important in both politics and business is to get the job done, and this applies first and foremost to the highest rulers: the cabinet. When the Dutch refer to the "government" (*regering*) they refer primarily to the cabinet rather than all branches of government or the entire administration. The government or cabinet must do the job of governing. The corollary to this is that others, specifically the parties in parliament, must allow them to govern. To be sure, the cabinet or individual ministers may be challenged and criticized but only with decent and polite restraint. The cabinet must not be harassed.

Parliament, that is, the two chambers of the States-General, is theoretically sovereign. The principle that the cabinet is entirely dependent on the confidence of parliament was firmly established in the protracted battle between the Second Chamber and the cabinet from 1866 to 1868. The Second Chamber repeatedly passed motions of censure against the cabinet and voted down the cabinet's budget proposals. The cabinet tried to maintain itself in office by twice dissolv-

19 *Ibid.* (February 1, 1964), quoted in Dick Schaap and Bert Pasterkamp, *De zaak Irene* (Amsterdam: ABC-Boeken, 1964), p. 68.

ing the chamber, but the newly-elected chambers still had strong majorities opposed to the cabinet. In the end, the cabinet resigned and was replaced by a new cabinet that had the chamber's confidence. Parliamentarism had triumphed. Furthermore, the constitutional provision that "the laws are inviolable" means that the judiciary is not allowed to test the constitutionality of laws passed by the States-General. Judicial review is unknown.[20] In this respect, too, parliament is fully sovereign.

It is impossible, therefore, to apply the concept of separation of powers to the relationship between cabinet and parliament. Yet, in practice, the cabinet enjoys a large measure of independence, based on the attitude that it is the government's task to govern. This "semiseparation of powers" is based not on constitutional provisions but on informal, but nonetheless deeply ingrained political practice. The semi-independent position of the cabinet is reinforced by the prevalent concept that cabinets are King's or Queen's cabinets, although they are all, at least after 1868, parliamentary cabinets, and by the strong tradition that membership in the cabinet is not compatible with membership in the States-General. Ministers have special reserved seats in the chambers and they may speak there, but they are not members and may not vote. Also, cabinet members have traditionally been recruited primarily from outside the States-General. Of the 334 ministers between 1848 and 1958, almost half never served in parliament and almost a fifth entered parliamentary service only after first having been on the cabinet; only slightly more than a third of the ministers had prior experience in parliament.[21] The semi-independence of the cabi-

[20] R. Kranenburg, *Het Nederlands staatsrecht* (8th ed., Haarlem: Tjeenk Willink, 1958), pp. 118–120, 288–293. See also J. V. Rijpperda Wierdsma, *Dualisme in ons staatsbestel* (Assen: Van Gorcum, 1961).

[21] Mattei Dogan and Maria Scheffer-Van der Veen, "Le personnel ministériel hollandais (1848–1958)," *L'Année Sociologique,* 3rd series, 1957–58, p. 100.

nets is further enhanced by the labels they frequently attach to themselves. Virtually all cabinets are based on a majority coalition in parliament, but many have described themselves as "extraparliamentary cabinets," "business cabinets," "crisis cabinets," and the like, thus emphasizing their autonomous status.

The practice of semiseparation of powers is eminently suited to the politics of accommodation. Dutch cabinets are egalitarian bodies. The prime minister stands out only slightly above his colleagues; the title prime minister (*Minister President*) did not even exist officially until 1945. The person charged with the formation of a new cabinet does not necessarily become its prime minister. In 1948, J. R. H. van Schaik formed the cabinet, but W. Drees became its prime minister and Van Schaik himself took the vice-premiership and the less exalted official title of minister without portfolio. Again, in 1951, Drees became the head of a new cabinet formed by someone else: C. P. M. Romme, who did not enter the cabinet himself.[22] The prime minister is undoubtedly *primus inter pares* but without undue emphasis on *primus*. The parties joining in a cabinet coalition do not have to be afraid, therefore, of being dominated by the strongman of a different party.

Furthermore, cabinets have usually been based on broad majorities in the Second Chamber, especially after 1946. The major parties have ample opportunities to participate in cabinets, and if they do participate, to occupy a number of posts roughly proportional to their parliamentary strength. Not all major parties are permanently on the cabinet, of course. But being in opposition does not entail being excluded from the policy-making process. There is no sharp line between government and opposition parties. Major pieces of legislation are often passed with the help of some

[22] E. van Raalte, *De ontwikkeling van het minister-presidentschap in Nederland, België, Frankrijk, Engeland en enige andere landen* (Leyden: Universitaire Pers, 1954), pp. 24–26, 44–45.

"opposition" parties and with a "government" party voting against. The departmental budgets are usually approved by all major parties with only one or more of the splinter groups in the opposition.

The cabinet's semi-independent status and its flexible partnership with all major parties—representing the four blocs—in the Second Chamber, give it a dual function in the politics of accommodation. Because of its broad composition, it is another confederal organ *within* which accommodation takes place. At the same time, because of its autonomous position above parliament and the parties and its presumed impartiality, it acts collectively as a mediator or balancer *between* the rival groups in the process of accommodation. In its first role, it resembles the Social and Economic Council, although its tasks are more comprehensive. Its second role is epitomized by the fifteen cabinet-appointed neutral members in the Social and Economic Council who hold the balance of power that is divided proportionally among the blocs and equally between workers and employers. The rule of the government's right to govern on which its special position in the politics of accommodation is based, is therefore of great importance.

These informal, unwritten rules govern the political business in Holland. They may not always be scrupulously followed, and because they are stated in general terms, they may be subject to different interpretations, but they are sufficiently salient to be regarded as *the* rules of the game. They contribute much to the success of the elite's efforts to govern the divided nation.

Another effect of the rules is to make politics dull and to keep popular interest at low ebb. Especially the rules of secrecy, proportionality, and depoliticization keep much of the fire and excitement out of politics. It would be wrong to assume, however, that the dullness of Dutch politics must be attributed to a lack of issues and tensions. The opposite is true: potentially divisive issues and disintegrative tendencies are ever present, but they are carefully controlled. The lack of excitement does not reflect a nearly perfect consensus, but rather the elite's conscious and deliberate attempts to cope with the system's fragility. Hence popular apathy and disinterest in politics and its apparent dullness have a positive value.

Chapter VIII
ACCOMMODATION
AND DEFERENCE

One of the problems of leadership in the politics of accommodation is the establishment of fruitful cooperation with the leaders of the rival blocs. The rules of the game regulate their mutual negotiations and search for compromises. The other major challenge of leadership concerns their relations with their followers. How can the leaders make concessions to other blocs without alienating their own people? The rules of secrecy and depoliticization perform a valuable function in this respect. But there are additional factors that can explain how the leaders maintain the confidence and allegiance of their followers.

IDEOLOGY AND OLIGARCHY

In contrast to the pragmatic tone of the accommodation process at the elite level, communications between the leaders and their followers tend to be couched in ideological terms. For instance, in their election manifestoes of 1963, all three large religious parties include references to Christian principles in the first plank. The Catholic party proclaims that it wants to "give form and content to the society of tomorrow based on the Christian view of life." The Christian Historical Union states its conviction that "God's Word" must be the "foundation and guideline" in policy-making. The Anti-Revolutionary party affirms as the first of the "principal points of a policy that will serve our people and the world": "the recognition of God's Majesty in and above the present tumultuous events and of man's dependence on His mercy in Jesus Christ, and also the requirement of obedience to His commandments."[1] The party's newspaper *Trouw* also reminds its readers of the basic Anti-Revolutionary political tenets, that is, opposition to the principles of the French Revolution. Divine sovereignty, and not popular sovereignty and self-determination, should be adhered to. A 1961 editorial spoke of the "objectionable doctrine of popular sovereignty" and an editorial in 1964 criticized the ideas of "liberty, equality, and fraternity springing forth from the unbelief of the French Revolution."[2]

The Labor party announces in its statement of principles adopted in 1959 that it will fight against the "still strong capitalistic forces . . . which cause economic exploitation and insecurity and spell cultural discrimination against large groups of the population." Furthermore, "ownership of the means of production should be subordinated to the welfare of the community as a whole" although wholesale nationalization is rejected. The Liberal platform of 1963 is filled with the ideas of "liberty" and "individual initiative," but specifi-

[1] Quoted in P. Goossen, *Parlement en Kiezer: 1963–1964* (The Hague: Nijhoff, 1963), pp. 99, 118, 173.

[2] *Trouw* (October 17, 1961; August 18, 1964). See also Adrianus C. de Ruiter, *De grenzen van de overheidstaak in de antirevolutionaire staatsleer* (Kampen: J. H. Kok, 1961).

cally rejects the nineteenth-century laissez-faire tradition.[3] The bulk of the programs of the five main parties deals with specific issues rather than general principles, however. Their programs are also much less ideological and more moderate in tone than those of the splinter parties.

Nevertheless, even on specific issues, communication between elite and mass reflects much more the ideological polarization at the mass level than the high degree of pragmatism and moderation at the top. On social and economic issues like the "bigness" of the central government, social security, and progressive taxation. Andries Hoogerwerf found a sharp contrast between the near-unanimity among the policy-making elites and the still considerable differences among both the formally stated goals of the parties in their platforms and among the opinions of the voters, as ascertained by sample surveys. The divergence was particularly wide between Socialists and Liberals with the religious parties, as expected, falling in the middle.[4]

The bloc leaders also maintain firm control over their political and social organizations. Ever since Michels' formulation of the "iron law of oligarchy," elite dominance of large-scale organizations has been an established doctrine in the social sciences, and the Dutch parties, labor unions, employers associations, and so on, confirm the strong tendency to oligarchical control. The elites' domination over their political parties is further strengthened by the Dutch electoral system for the politically most important Second Chamber: a list system of proportional representation in which, for all practical purposes, the entire country serves as a single constituency. Because of the stability of voting patterns, the election of a particular candidate is virtually determined by his rank on the list. Vacancies occurring between parliamentary

[3] Quoted in Goossen, pp. 185, 204–205.
[4] A. Hoogerwerf, "Sociaal-politieke strijdpunten: Smeulend vuur," *Sociologische Gids*, Vol. 10, No. 5 (September–October 1963), pp. 261–262.

elections are also filled in this way; no by-elections are necessary.

The composition of almost the entire Second Chamber is
therefore determined by those who make up the electoral lists
of the parties: the party elites. The selection of candidates
is purely an internal party matter. Only one out of every
seven or eight supporters of the large parties is a dues-paying
party member. The Catholic and Anti-Revolutionary parties
have relatively large memberships: about one out of every
five voters is also a member. The membership ratios of the
other parties are much lower: about 1 to 10 for the Christian Historical Union, 1 to 12 for the Labor party, and 1 to
21 for the Liberals.[5] More than 85 per cent of the voters do
not even have a nominal voice in the composition of the party lists. And the actual influence of the relatively few rank
and file members is not much greater. There is no general law
that governs the selection of candidates and each party has
its own rules. These rules are usually based on at least some
degree of democratic choice, but in reality the highest governing councils of the parties have the last word.

The almost half a million members of the Catholic party,
for instance, can participate in the selection process first at
the local level, by suggesting possible candidates whose
names are then sent up to higher levels of the party hierarchy.
At the very top, the lists are decided upon by a special "election council" where the party's central executive committee
has the majority of the votes. These lists are then submitted
to the rank and file for their approval of the ranking of the
candidates on the lists. The individual member's power to
make changes is extremely limited. He can give a preferential

[5] Georg Geismann, *Politische Struktur und Regierungssystem in
den Niederlanden*, Kölner Schriften zur Politischen Wissenschaft,
Vol. 4 (Frankfurt am Main and Bonn: Athenäum Verlag, 1964), p.
66 n.; R. van Dijk and G. Kuiper, *Gestalten en getijden in de sociale
werkelijkheid: Een oriëntering* (Amersfoort: Roelofs van Goor,
1964), p. 49.

vote to only one candidate, and the candidate in question must amass an enormous number of these preferential votes in order to move higher on the list: the second candidate must get more than 50 per cent in order to move into first place, and 33.3 per cent of the preferential votes are required to effect a change from the number three to the number two spot, and so on—not an impossible requirement, but highly improbable. This is not yet the whole story. The party's election council is empowered to determine the final composition of one-third of all those high positions on the list which appear to guarantee election. These candidates whose virtual certainty of being elected is supposed to assure that the party delegation to the Second Chamber "should reflect the varied social and regional composition of the Catholic Party as much as possible," cannot be touched by the rank and file at all.[6] Even without these strict safeguards, oligarchical control of the party would not be in great danger, but the Catholic leaders take no chances!

The other parties do not have the same elaborate rules, but their practices are similar. Elite domination is the pattern everywhere. This does not mean that the party leaders are prone to disregard the interests of either their members or their voters, or to use their extraordinary powers for nepotism and corruption.[7] The "oligarchs" attempt to make the party lists as attractive and representative as possible, although always within the confines of co-optation from the established leadership of the bloc.

On election day the voters can either vote for the first candidate of their party, which is in effect a vote for the entire

[6] I. Lipschits, "De politieke partij en de selectie van candidaten," *Sociologische Gids*, Vol. 10, No. 5 (September–October 1963), pp. 274–278. See also Linda C. Wilson, "Politics of the Dutch Party System: The Impact of New Guinea" (unpublished master's thesis, University of California, Berkeley, 1963), pp. 64–75.

[7] R. Kranenburg, *Politieke organisatie en groepspsychologie* (Haarlem: Tjeenk Willink, 1956), pp. 51–61.

party list as presented to them, but they also have the right to
cast their ballot for somebody who is lower on the list. And a
candidate may be elected if he receives a sufficient number
of preferential votes. After the first parliamentary election
held under the proportional representation system in 1918,
seven members entered the hundred-member Second Chamber as a result of preferential election. This loophole was
soon closed. In 1921 the electoral law was amended and a
high minimum was established for election by preferential
vote. Under the new provision only one of the seven could
have been elected in 1918.[8] The voters were not completely
deprived of their power to bring about some change in the
party lists, but a successful exercise of this power is most unlikely. In the Catholic party—more openly oligarchical than
the other parties—even this slight risk has been eliminated.
Every candidate has to sign a statement "that, if he should
be elected by preferential votes in the official election, he will
not accept a seat in the Second Chamber except by permission of the party's central executive committee."[9]

DEFERENCE

　　Neither the ideologically stylized pattern of
elite-mass communications nor the high degree of elite dominance of the bloc organizations can fully explain the persistent allegiance of the rank and file of the blocs to their leaders. The people must have an inherently strong tendency to
be obedient and allegiant—regardless of particular circumstances. This tendency will be referred to as *deference*. This
term is here used in its broadest meaning: an individual's
acceptance of his position both in the social hierarchy and on
the scale of political authority, accompanied by a low level

[8] P. J. Oud, *Het jongste verleden: Parlementaire geschiedenis van
Nederland 1918–1940*, 6 vols. (Assen: Van Gorcum, 1948–51), Vol.
1, pp. 321–322.
[9] Quoted in Lipschits, p. 277.

of participation and interest in politics. For the masses this entails respect for and submission to their superiors. These deferential attitudes are strong among the Dutch. Hans Daalder, the most astute observer of the Dutch political scene, speaks of the "mixture of both deference and indifference which has tended to characterize the attitude of most Dutchmen toward authority."[10]

When confronted with the question: "All of us have ideas about what people should be like. Here is a list of characteristics you might find in people. Could you select the quality you admire most?"—a large number of Dutch respondents chose "respectful, doesn't overstep his place" (in Dutch: "heeft eerbied, weet zijn plaats"). This question was borrowed from Almond and Verba's *Civic Culture* study. A comparison of the Dutch answers with the answers in the United Kingdom, Germany, Italy, and the United States produces some striking contrasts (see Table 22).[11] In Holland, 19 per cent chose "respectful," a much higher percentage than in any of the other four countries: about twice as high as in Britain, Italy, and the United States, and almost four times the unexpectedly low 5 per cent in Germany. Two other qualities received many more favorable mentions in Holland than in any of the other four countries: "active in public and social affairs" and "ambitious, wants to get ahead." Both can be interpreted as indicators of deferential attitudes: respect for the elite's public service role and admiration for their high position on the social and political ladders. Such

[10] Hans Daalder, "The Netherlands: Opposition in a Segmented Society," in Robert A. Dahl, ed., *Political Oppositions in Western Democracies* (New Haven: Yale University Press, 1966), p. 197.

[11] The percentages in Table 22 differ from those in Gabriel A. Almond and Sidney Verba, *The Civic Culture: Political Attitudes and Democracy in Five Nations* (Princeton: Princeton University Press, 1963), p. 265, because they represent the *one* characteristic that the respondents admired most rather than the *two* most admired qualities. Almond and Verba used the answers to both the question cited above and the follow-up question: "Which would be next?"

TABLE 22.   MOST ADMIRED QUALITIES IN FIVE COUNTRIES

(In per cent)

Quality	Netherlands (1,600)	United Kingdom (963)	Germany (955)	Italy (995)	United States (970)
Does his job well	14	15	16	29	14
Active in public and social affairs	7	3	4	4	2
Ambitious, wants to get ahead	22	11	12	8	12
Generous, considerate of others	12	49	26	14	39
Thrifty, saving	9	4	18	9	3
Lets no one take advantage of him	1	2	2	3	2
Keeps himself to himself	13	5	12	16	15
Respectful, doesn't overstep his place	19	9	5	10	11
Don't know	4	2	6	8	2

an interpretation is in accord with the impressionistic finding that deference is strong and widespread in Holland, but it does not constitute independent evidence, of course. Ambition and the desire to get ahead may operate in the context of acceptance of the political and social hierarchy and may represent no more than a person's desire to rise within his own well-defined social station, but it may just as well indicate the much stronger desire to break through class barriers and to reject political tutelage.

One other contrast stands out. Generosity and considerateness are chosen by far fewer Dutchmen than by the respondents in the other four countries. The 14 per cent figure for Italy is only slightly higher than Holland's 12 per cent, but the percentages for Germany, the United States, and Britain are respectively more than two, three, and four times higher. The Dutch are clearly deficient in these attitudes which Almond and Verba describe as "protocivic" or "precivic"—qualities of the greatest importance to an effectively functioning democracy.[12] This finding only indicates an attitude among the people as a whole, of course, and not among the elite. At the elite level, mutual considerateness is strong and plays a vital role in the process of accommodation. It is interesting that admiration for considerateness and generosity rises with socioeconomic status. In the two higher groups (A and B) the percentages are 18 and 16 compared with 9 and 10 for the two lower socioeconomic groups (C and D).

Admiration for the quality of "respect"—indicative of deferential attitudes—is high in Holland among all groups, but especially in the Calvinist bloc. Table 23 shows the percentages choosing "respect" as the most admired of the eight qualities among the members of the three blocs and among the supporters of the five main parties. The highest percentages occur among the Calvinists and their parties. The figures for the other groups are considerably lower, but they remain

---

[12] Almond and Verba, p. 266.

at a higher level than the totals in the other four countries.

One important reason for the great latitude the Dutch tend to accord to their leaders is their strong belief that the leaders should serve the general interest rather than the special interest of their own bloc. In a 1954 poll, the respondents were asked what they thought the task of their representatives in the Second Chamber was. Only 11 per cent of the answers to this open-ended question could be classified under the heading of "protection of the interests of their own voters." Almost three times as many respondents (30 per cent) thought that the legislators should look after the interests of the Dutch people as a whole, and many others implied the same: promoting the country's welfare, making laws in the public interest, represent the entire people, and so on.[13] This strong approval of serving the public interest gives the leaders the flexibility to compromise and even violate, if nec-

TABLE 23. RESPECT AS MOST ADMIRED QUALITY BY
PARTIES AND RELIGIOUS BLOCS

Party or Bloc	Per cent	(Number)
Catholic	13	(333)
Labor	18	(469)
Liberal	19	(142)
Anti-Revolutionary	32	(143)
Chr. Hist. Union	28	(148)
Other parties	18	(85)
Catholic bloc	16	(389)
Secular bloc	17	(873)
Calvinist bloc	28	(308)
Total sample	19	(1600)

[13] Nederlands Instituut voor de Publieke Opinie, *De Nederlandse kiezer: Een onderzoek naar zijn gedragingen en opvattingen* (The Hague: Staatsdrukkerij- en Uitgeverijbedrijf, 1956), p. 45.

essary, their bloc interests in the process of accommodation. This attitude, incidentally, also softens somewhat the finding of lack of considerateness and generosity among the Dutch, as noted above.

The Dutch have largely been satisfied with the established political and social organizations. The incidence of individual affiliation with voluntary associations is high. In the *Civic Culture* survey, the following question was included: "Are you a member of any organizations now—trade or labor unions, business organizations, social groups, professional or farm organizations, cooperatives, fraternal or veterans' groups, athletic clubs, political, charitable, civic or religious organizations, or any other organized group? Which ones?"[14] A quite similar and therefore comparable question was included in a Dutch survey conducted in 1955 and 1956. The only major difference is that the question in Holland referred only to *active* membership. This must have lowered the percentage of affiliation considerably. On the other hand, the percentage obtained in Holland was raised because the sample included persons of 12 years of age and older whereas the *Civic Culture* samples were drawn from 18 year old and older people. Because organizational membership in Holland was especially high in the 12 to 18 year group, their inclusion inflated the total percentage to some extent.[15]

Table 24 shows the incidence of organizational membership in Holland and four other countries. Exactly one half of all Dutchmen belong to some organization, and 18 per cent belong to more than one. These percentages are quite high compared with the other four countries. Dutchmen appear

[14] Almond and Verba, p. 301 n.

[15] Centraal Bureau voor de Statistiek, *Vrije-tijdsbesteding in Nederland Winter 1955/'56: Deel 5, Verenigingsleven* (Zeist: De Haan, 1957), pp. 8–13, 32. The average number of participations by members in group activities was 62. If the 12 to 18 year age group had been excluded, the total percentage of affiliation would have been reduced from 50 per cent to about 47 per cent.

to be joiners to about the same extent as the British, less than
the Americans, but slightly more than the Germans and considerably more than the Italians.[16]

These high percentages of affiliation suggest the existence
of widespread acceptance of and satisfaction with the existing associations, although they do not fully prove it. In the
Dutch example, this interpretation appears to be correct,
however. The Dutch are not only joiners; they also have a
strong tendency to rely on groups for political action. This
habit is shown in the responses of the Dutch sample to another (open-ended) question borrowed from the *Civic Culture* questionnaire: "Suppose a law were being considered by
the States-General (that is, the Second and First Chambers)

TABLE 24.   ORGANIZATIONAL MEMBERSHIP IN FIVE COUNTRIES
(In per cent)

Membership	Nether- lands	United Kingdom	Germany	Italy	United States
Nonmembers	50	53	56	71	43
Members	50	47	44	29	57
Single memberships	*32*	*31*	*32*	*24*	*25*
Multiple memberships	*18*	*16*	*12*	*6*	*32*

SOURCE: Adapted from Centraal Bureau voor de Statistiek, *Vrije-
tijdsbesteding in Nederland Winter 1955/'56: Deel 5, Verenigingsleven* (Zeist: De Haan, 1957), p. 10, and Gabriel A. Almond and
Sidney Verba, *The Civic Culture: Political Attitudes and Democracy
in Five Nations* (Princeton: Princeton University Press, 1963), pp.
302, 320.

[16] Also more than the French, among whom only 41 per cent are
organization members and 59 per cent nonmembers. See Arnold M.
Rose, "Voluntary Associations in France," in *Theory and Method in
the Social Sciences* (Minneapolis: University of Minnesota Press,
1954), pp. 84–85. In Norway, about two-thirds of all adults belong
to associations. See Harry Eckstein, *Division and Cohesion in Democracy: A Study of Norway* (Princeton: Princeton University
Press, 1966), p. 104.

that you considered to be very unjust or harmful? What do you think you could do?" Table 25 gives the results. First, 54 per cent do not feel competent to do anything at all: they either do not know what they would do or explicitly state that they would do nothing. More than half of the Dutch respondents would simply resign themselves to such potentially harmful or unjust action. The percentage of passivity is considerably higher than in the United States (25 per cent) and the United Kingdom (38 per cent), and not strikingly lower than in Germany (63 per cent). Second, the strategies employed by those Dutchmen who indicated they would take some action, also differ in a number of interesting respects from the other countries. In all four other countries, individual action is mentioned more frequently than collective action, but not in Holland. The Dutch shy away from direct contact with political leaders: only 7 per cent would follow this course of action, compared with no less than 57 per cent of the Americans, 44 per cent of the British, and 12 per cent of the Germans. Only the Italians match the Dutch reluctance to take up individual contact with political leaders. The individual action the Dutch seem to prefer is to cast a protest vote in the secrecy and anonymity of the voting booth.

The strategies that entail attempts to enlist the aid of others also show interesting differences between the Dutch and the other four groups. Many Dutchmen (16 per cent) would try to get some kind of ad hoc informal group together. This is a much smaller percentage than the 29 per cent of the Americans who would resort to informal group action, but only slightly lower than the 18 per cent in the United Kingdom. The Germans and Italians rank much lower on the scale. On the other hand, the Dutch are more likely than any of the other groups to rely on already existing organizations like political parties, labor unions, churches, and other formal groups to which they belong: 7 per cent would work through a party, and 7 per cent through another formal group. The figures for Germany are close to the Dutch per-

TABLE 25. COOPERATIVE COMPETENCE IN FIVE COUNTRIES

Cooperative competence	Nether-lands (1,600)	United Kingdom (963)	Germany (955)	Italy (995)	United States (970)
Try to Enlist Aid of Others					
Organize an informal group; arouse friends and neighbors, get them to write letters of protest or to sign a petition	16	18	7	6	29
Work through a political party	7	2	6	2	1
Work through a formal group (union, church, professional) to which they belong	7	3	7	2	4
Act Alone					
Directly contact political leaders (elected officials) or the press; write a letter to or visit a local political leader	7	44	12	7	57

TABLE 25. *(continued)*

Cooperative competence	Nether-lands (1,600)	United Kingdom (963)	Germany (955)	Italy (995)	United States (970)
Directly contact administrative (nonelected) officials	1	1	4	4	0
Consult a lawyer; appeal through courts	0	0	1	1	0
Vote against offending officials at next election	8	3	4	1	7
Take some violent action	2	0	2	1	0
Just protest	4	0	0	3	0
Other	1	2	0	2	0
Do Nothing	43	32	56	50	21
Don't Know	11	6	7	22	4
Total	107	111	106	101	123

NOTE: Percentages of more than 100 are due to multiple responses.
SOURCE: Adapted from Almond and Verba, *The Civic Culture*, p. 203.

centages, but those for the other three countries are much lower. In their reliance on informal groups, the Dutch resemble the British; in their reliance on formal organizations, they are more like the Germans.

In Tables 26 and 27, the results are cross-tabulated with bloc membership and party preference. On the whole, the groups do not differ much from each other in their choice of political strategy. The Calvinists, and the Anti-Revolutionaries in particular, would rely on their political party more than the others. The Liberals tend to rely little on other formal organizations—few Liberals belong to a union or are devoted churchmen—but they are, like the Anti-Revolutionaries, more likely to take informal group action than the others. The Anti-Revolutionaries are the least passive of all the groups, possibly as a result of their strong moral principles which do not allow them to respond to a proposed "unjust" rule with inaction. The differences within Holland are less striking than those across national boundaries. On the basis of cross-national comparisons one can safely conclude that the Dutch are relatively passive even when faced with the possibility of grave political injustice or injury. They are also reluctant to take overt action as individuals. But when they do act, they usually resort to a collective effort, often through an already existing organization. These tendencies—especially the relatively low degree of activism and the relatively high reliance on established associations—lend strong support to the contention that the Dutch are highly deferential in their political attitudes.

The extent of popular satisfaction with the existing party system, including the oligarchical organization of the parties, is also shown by the results of a survey held in 1954. Large majorities are happy to leave almost everything up to the parties. Only 32 per cent consider it important to know personally the candidate they vote for, and almost twice as many (59 per cent) do not regard this as important. Should candidates engage in door-to-door campaigning in order to give

TABLE 26.   RELIGIOUS BLOCS AND COOPERATIVE COMPETENCE

Cooperative competence	Bloc			Total (N=1,600)
	Catholic (389)	Secular (873)	Calvinist (308)	
Try to Enlist Aid of Others				
Informal group, etc.	15	16	17	16
Political party	6	5	12	7
Formal group	8	6	9	7
Act Alone				
Contact political leaders, etc.	7	6	11	7
Contact administrative officials	1	1	2	1
Consult lawyer, etc.	0	0	0	0
Vote against officials	7	9	5	8
Violent action	1	3	1	2
Just protest	4	3	5	4
Other	1	1	0	1
Do Nothing	44	47	32	43
Don't know	11	10	15	11
Total	105	106	110	107

NOTE: Percentages of more than 100 are due to multiple responses.

TABLE 27. PARTY PREFERENCE AND COOPERATIVE COMPETENCE

Cooperative competence	Party							
	Catholic (333)	Labor (469)	Liberal (142)	Anti-Rev. (143)	Chr. Hist. Union (148)	Other (85)	Don't know (280)	Total (1,600)
Try to Enlist Aid of Others								
Informal group, etc.	15	14	25	22	15	15	11	16
Political party	7	6	7	12	8	6	5	7
Formal group	9	8	1	9	7	7	5	7
Act Alone								
Contact political leaders	9	7	7	11	9	7	4	7
Contact admin. officials	1	1	1	1	1	2	0	1
Consult lawyer, etc.	0	0	0	0	0	0	0	0
Vote against officials	8	10	11	6	6	6	5	8
Violent action	2	3	3	2	1	2	0	2
Just protest	4	3	5	4	3	2	5	4
Other	0	1	3	1	1	0	1	1
Do Nothing	43	41	39	31	41	51	55	43
Don't Know	12	13	2	11	14	12	12	11
Total	110	107	104	110	106	110	103	107

NOTE: Percentages of more than 100 are due to multiple responses.

the voters a chance to get to know them? Again, only 29 per cent approve of this idea, and 55 per cent disapprove. And only 4 per cent of the respondents have ever tried to write or speak to their representatives in the Second Chamber; 96 per cent have never had any contact. What do the Dutch think of the practice of nullifying a preferential vote for a candidate low on his party's electoral list by party fiat, as in the Catholic party? A majority (52 per cent) indeed do not like this idea, but no less than 26 per cent even go along with this degree of elite domination. Actually few voters use their right to cast a preferential vote: less than 10 per cent in the 1963 elections.[17]

Dutch workers are equally deferential to the labor-union leaders, in spite of the leaders' great moderation in their dealings with employers. Strikes have been rare after the First World War, even during the depression. In 1931, 850,000 labor days were lost, and more than twice this number in 1932.[18] From then on the situation changed, although conservative cabinets with little interest in social welfare and economic planning predominated. Labor-union leaders kept the number of days lost in strikes down to an average of little more than 100,000 per year during the rest of the decade, although labor's bargaining power was weak and the unions could not achieve great gains for their members. After the Second World War, Dutch reconstruction was helped immeasurably by the moderate aims of the unions and their re-

[17] Nederlands Instituut voor de Publieke Opinie, *De Nederlandse kiezer*, pp. 42, 54, 56, 67. See also H. Daudt and J. Stapel, "Parlement, politiek en kiezer: Verslag van een opinie-onderzoek," *Acta Politica*, Vol. 1, Nos. 1–4 (1965–66), pp. 46–76. In 1956, almost 20 per cent of all preferential votes were cast for female candidates, probably mainly by women. See Jacqueline C. Schokking, *De vrouw in de Nederlandse politiek: Een inleidend onderzoek* (Assen: Van Gorcum, 1958), pp. 76–77.

[18] H. Hoefnagels, *Een eeuw sociale problematiek: Van sociaal conflict naar strategische samenwerking* (Assen: Van Gorcum, 1957), p. 223.

luctance to strike. And the members by and large acquiesced. Both officially sponsored strikes and unofficial wildcat strikes occurred less frequently than elsewhere. As W. F. de Gaay Fortman, professor of labor law at Amsterdam's Free University, states, the Dutch workers "can feel at ease with the leadership given by the three large trade-union federations, which have the aim of negotiating with employers as long as possible to reach agreement."[19]

The Burkean dilemma of whether an elected official should be a representative or a delegate is not a dilemma in Holland. Leaders lead; followers follow. This is also reflected in the formal constitutional structure. As compared with direct democracy, the Dutch system is the acme of representative democracy. Only the local and provincial legislatures and one house of the national legislature are elected directly by the people. The ballot, though it is a large sheet of paper, is a "short ballot": only one choice can be made. Elections take place, on the average, less than once a year. Referendum and recall do not exist. In the judicial process, juries are never used. Nonetheless, this system has long been popularly accepted without a question or significant protest.

Persistent deference depends on a dual relationship, of course. The Frenchman's view of his government is well stated in D. W. Brogan's words: the state is "not a referee but a player—and probably a dirty player."[20] The Dutch attitude is markedly different: he respects and trusts his leaders. But the quality of leadership does have a great deal to do with this. The Dutch leaders are not "dirty players." They do not violate their followers' trust. Sometimes they try to reinforce the obedience of the rank and file by stern moral lectures. For example, the 1954 pastoral letter by the Catholic bishops warned against the "spirit of criticism" and admon-

[19] W. F. de Gaay Fortman, "Industrial Relations in the Netherlands," *Delta*, Vol. 3, No. 3 (Autumn 1960), p. 30.
[20] Quoted in Philip Williams, *Crisis and Compromise: Politics in the Fourth Republic* (Hamden, Conn.: Archon Books, 1964), p. 7.

ished all Catholics not to "overestimate their own opinions" and to recognize the "good intentions of their own leaders."[21] But the elite are mainly successful in maintaining the people's allegiance because they do in fact manage to satisfy their expectations.

It is remarkable, nevertheless, that popular deference is sufficiently strong to survive an occasional confrontation between the elite and the rank and file. One such instance occurred in 1964. The episode is particularly revealing because the split between the leaders and the people was very deep and because the issue was considered of major importance by both sides. A private company built a small artificial island in the North Sea just outside Dutch territorial waters, and consequently, it was hoped, outside Dutch government jurisdiction. A commercial television station was built on the island which began transmitting its programs in the summer of 1964 to the densely populated western part of the country. The programs of the pirate station were especially welcome in this area; foreign stations (British, Belgian, French, and German) could not be received, and viewers were entirely dependent on the programs of the one Dutch station. Interest in the new venture was great: in August, 94 per cent of the people had heard or read about it. The North Sea station was enormously popular in the area it covered. A survey in November discovered that it could easily compete with the Dutch station, and indeed often had a larger audience. Its most popular programs were viewed on more than 50 per cent of the sets within reach. In order to be able to get a better reception of the North Sea station's programs—its transmitter was relatively weak—many people installed additional and costly antennas on their roofs. In August, 7 per cent of all households with television had such a special antenna, and the percentage rose to 12 in September, 15 in October, and 17 in November.

[21] Bisschoppelijk mandement, *De Katholiek in het openbare leven van deze tijd* (Utrecht: 1954), p. 37.

TABLE 28. POPULARITY OF THE NORTH SEA TELEVISION STATION, 1964
(In per cent)

Opinion	February	May	June	August
Opposed to government action against the station	62	60	61	70
In favor of government action against the station	15	17	14	11
No opinion	23	23	25	19

SOURCE: Nederlands Instituut voor de Publieke Opinie, *Bericht No. 1011* (August 28, 1964).

The new television station was as unwelcome to the leaders as it was welcome to the people, because it threatened the elite's firm and exclusive control over the air waves. Thus far Dutch television programs had been monopolized by the radio and television associations of the four blocs. Only the Liberals, who have no formal connection with the Liberal broadcast organization, were less deeply concerned. Table 28 shows that the people were overwhelmingly opposed to any government actions against the North Sea station. When the programs began in the summer, public opinion favored their unhindered continuation by an almost seven to one margin. The government and the parties were not deterred. A law to kill the station, cleverly contrived in terms of international law, was enacted by a vote of 114 to 9 in the Second Chamber. Only the Liberals, the small Farmers party, and one Laborite cast negative votes. The vote in the First Chamber was equally lopsided: 57 to 9. Here only the Liberals and the Pacifists were in the opposition. On December 17, the government occupied the island and ended its programs.

How did the people react to this? In a poll conducted in late December, about two-thirds of those who used to watch the North Sea station's programs said they now missed them. But a strong majority of all people also basically approved the government's action in view of the passage of the enabling legislation by the Chambers: the popular verdict was 43 to 33 in favor of the government with 24 per cent undecided.[22] On a major and deeply felt issue, the elite man-

[22] Nederlands Instituut voor de Publieke Opinie, *Bericht No. 1011* (August 28, 1964), *No. 1026* (December 7, 1964), and *No. 1033* (January 12, 1965). On another major issue, withdrawal from Indonesia in 1949 and West Irian in 1962, the government also acted clearly against public opinion. The treaty that granted independence to Indonesia was opposed by 33 per cent, approved by 21 per cent, with 46 per cent undecided. Yet the two chambers voted their approval with better than two-thirds majorities. See Arend Lijphart, *The Trauma of Decolonization: The Dutch and West New Guinea* (New Haven: Yale University Press, 1966), pp. 114–124, 247–249, 283–284.

aged not only to defy public opinion, but to do so with the people's approval. Deference may be a too weak term to describe this attitude to authority; perhaps one ought to speak of "docility."

THE SPLINTER PARTIES

Another measure of deference is the degree to which the people have continued supporting the five major political parties that rule the country. After the introduction of proportional representation, the election of splinter parties became easy. In 1918 only 0.5 per cent of the popular vote was needed in order to get a seat in the Second Chamber; one party managed to get its representative elected with a bare 0.508 per cent of the total vote![23] The required percentage was raised to 0.75 per cent in the four elections that followed and to a full 1 per cent after 1933. But it was lowered again to 0.67 per cent after the 1956 election when the Second Chamber increased in size from 100 to 150 members.[24] Yet the Dutch have kept supporting the established traditional parties in overwhelming numbers.

Table 29 shows the seats won by the minor parties and, for purposes of comparison, those won by the major parties in the Second Chamber. The "major" parties are the established parties, representing the four blocs, which regularly participate in cabinets: the Big Five after the Second World War and the Big Six in the interwar years (when there were two Liberal parties). The "minor" parties are those that do not belong to the establishment and are largely kept out of the process of accommodation. The major-minor distinction also implies a difference in size, although a minor party like

[23] Oud, *Het jongste verleden*, Vol. 1, p. 319.

[24] After 1933, another change was introduced into the electoral law which tended to give a slight advantage to the larger parties and a disadvantage to the smaller parties: the largest averages (d'Hondt) method of proportional representation replaced the largest remainders method.

TABLE 29. SECOND CHAMBER SEATS WON BY MINOR AND MAJOR PARTIES, 1918–1967

Parties	1918	1922	1925	1929	1933	1937	1946	1948	1952	1956	1959	1963	1967
Minor parties:													
Catholic	0	0	1	0	1	0	0	1	2	0	0	0	0
Protestant	2	1	3	4	5	4	2	2	2	2	3	4	4
Secular-leftist	4	2	1	2	5	3	10	8	6	4	5	8	16
Secular-rightist	7	3	1	2	2	4	0	0	0	0	0	3	7
All minor parties	13	6	6	8	13	11	12	11	10	6	8	15	27
Big Five/Six	87	94	94	92	87	89	88	89	90	94	142	135	123
Total seats	100	100	100	100	100	100	100	100	100	100	150	150	150

the Communists actually received more votes in the 1946
elections than two of the major parties (the Liberals and the
Christian Historical Union).

In spite of the ease of entry into the Second Chamber, the
minor parties have never been able to get many representatives elected until recently. In 1967, they won 27 of the 150
seats (18 per cent). Before 1967, the maximum percentage
they were able to win was 13: in the first election conducted
under proportional representation in 1918 and in the election of the depression year 1933. In the latter year of crisis,
no less than 48 minor parties sought election and 8 were successful in getting at least one seat. In 1963, they won a total
of fifteen seats, but these represented only 10 per cent of the
total in the expanded Second Chamber. In other words, the
established parties never held less than 87 per cent of all Second Chamber seats from 1918 until 1967.

The persistent strength of the Big Five of the parties is
even more significant because the minor parties aim their ap-
peals almost invariably at those voters who are disgruntled
about the major parties' moderation, tendency to compromise, and lack of ideological consistency. Formal pronounce-
ments by the leaders of the major parties in platforms and
editorials are often couched in terms of ideological principles, but the smaller parties are even more puristic doctri-
naires. The small parties easily fit the fourfold bloc pattern of
Dutch society (see Table 29). They represent the radical
fringes of the blocs: the extreme right of the generally conservative Liberal bloc, the extreme left of the Socialist bloc,
and the extremes on both the right and the left of the generally middle-of-the-road Catholic and Calvinist blocs. It is still
too early to evaluate the Democrats '66, the newest of the
splinter groups, but it has been classified among the secular-
leftist parties in the table.

The Catholic party has been troubled the least by splinter
groups operating on its right and left flanks. Before the Second World War, a leftist Roman Catholic People's party par-

ticipated in the elections but it gained only a single seat and only in 1925 and 1933. After the war, the ultraconservative and highly nationalistic Catholic National party was set up by former Catholic party member and former minister of colonies Ch. J. I. M. Welter. It represented the angry reaction of the most conservative elements in the Catholic bloc to their party's postwar colonial policy and its alliance with the Labor party. The Catholic Nationalists won one seat in 1948 and two in 1952, but they merged again with the main Catholic party after the episcopal letter of 1954 which urged Catholic unity.[25]

In the Calvinist bloc, political splintering has been stronger and more persistent. The left-wing Christian Democrats participated in all elections in the interwar years but gained seats only in 1918, 1933, and 1937. Most of the Protestant splinter parties have been on the extreme right, representing the most orthodox, fundamentalist, and anti-Catholic of the Calvinists. The Political Reformed party has been continually represented in the Second Chamber since 1922 with usually about two or three seats. The most recent right-wing Calvinist party is the Reformed Political League, representing a minuscule religious sect arising from yet another schism (in 1944) among orthodox Calvinists. It has polled a steady 0.6 to 0.7 per cent of the popular vote, and finally won a seat in 1963. In their platforms these parties condemn the other religious parties, including specifically the Anti-Revolutionary party and the Christian Historical Union "because they do not base their policies . . . on the Bible and on the doctrine of the Christian church." Their planks include such things as opposition to further integration into the predominantly Catholic "Little Europe," opposition to social security, secular public education, women's suffrage, compulsory vacci-

---

[25] See W. A. M. van Eekeren, "The Catholic People's Party in the Netherlands" (unpublished doctoral dissertation, Georgetown University, 1956), pp. 155–168.

nation, cremation, and the abolition of the death penalty—all on religious grounds.[26] The reaction of the Protestant parties to the news of Princess Irene's conversion to Catholicism was typical. The two major parties issued moderate and soothing statements, but the Political Reformed party's general conference sent a telegram of protest to Queen Juliana: the conversion was said to run counter to the country's history in which, "under the leadership of your illustrious ancestors, our nation was liberated from the power of Rome and Spain."[27]

Left-wing extremism in the Socialist bloc has been reflected by a large variety of splinter groups, but primarily by the Communists. Before the Second World War, the Communist party reached its peak with four seats in 1933. In the first postwar election, they increased their representation dramatically to ten seats, but they have gone steadily downhill since then. In 1963 they even collected fewer votes than the Pacifist Socialist party, another dissident left-wing party founded in 1957. The latter party is both pacifist (e.g., opposed to Holland's membership in N.A.T.O.) and Socialist in the doctrinaire sense. It goes much further than the Labor party, for instance, in demanding collective ownership of all means of production, transportation services, banks, and insurance companies.[28]

Finally, the leadership of the Liberal bloc has had relatively few challenges from right-wing splinter parties. The seven seats won by rightist secular groups in 1918 do not accurately reflect dissension within the Liberal bloc because five of these seven seats were gained by small parties that merged with one of the large Liberal parties in 1921. Fascist parties never made important gains. The semifascist League

[26] Goossen, *Parlement en Kiezer: 1963–64*, pp. 125–133, 194–196.

[27] Quoted in Dick Schaap and Bert Pasterkamp, *De zaak Irene* (Amsterdam: ABC-Boeken, 1964), p. 49.

[28] L. van der Land, *Het ontstaan van de Pacifistisch Socialistische Partij* (Amsterdam: Bezige Bij, 1962), esp. pp. 24–46. See also Frits Kool, "Communism in Holland: A Study in Futility," *Problems of Communism*, Vol. 9, No. 5 (September–October 1960), pp. 17–24.

for National Recovery won only one seat in 1933, and the Dutch National Socialist party received four seats in 1937. Other groups classified as rightist secular parties have been mainly special interest parties. The present Farmers party started this way, but it has developed into a party of protest against the high taxes, governmental "regimentation," and other burdens of economic planning and the welfare state. Not only farmers support it: in the 1966 municipal elections in not so rural Amsterdam, they won almost ten per cent of the total vote!

These splinter parties on the radical fringes of the four blocs have never been able to make significant inroads into the overwhelming control of the government by the moderate parties of the establishment. An even better indicator of the deference of the people to their bloc leaders is the steady positive support they have given the major parties at the polls. Table 30 presents not only the votes for the major and the minor parties but also the extent of nonvoting and invalid ballots in all elections for which these figures are available. Absenteeism has always been low, partly as a result of the compulsory voting law though it is not seriously enforced. Few people cast invalid votes by abstaining or spoiling their ballots. Support for minor parties has been around 10 per cent with an all-time high of almost 20 per cent in 1967. Votes for the minor parties can be interpreted as either antisystem or antiestablishment votes. Assuming that the same interpretation is valid for those failing to vote and those casting invalid ballots—a most pessimistic assumption—one can still reach the conclusion that since 1925 the major parties have never received less than the positive expression of support of *three-fourths of all eligible voters* except in 1967. Even then, the Big Five did not fall too far below this mark with a total of 72.7 per cent.

Daalder regards the occurrence of splinter parties as a "dysfunctional strain" in the system,[29] but it would be wrong

---

[29] Daalder, In Dahl, ed., *Political Oppositions*, p. 225.

TABLE 30.   NONVOTERS, INVALID BALLOTS AND VOTES FOR THE MAJOR AND MINOR PARTIES, 1925–1967

(In per cent)

Registered Voters	1925	1929	1933	1937	1946	1948	1952	1956	1959	1963	1967
Nonvoters	8.6	7.3	5.5	5.6	6.9	6.3	5.0	4.5	4.4	4.9	5.3
Invalid ballots	4.3	4.3	4.4	3.5	2.9	2.9	2.9	2.0	2.3	2.3	2.5
Minor parties	10.1	9.5	14.4	14.0	12.4	11.8	12.2	7.9	7.8	11.6	19.6
Big Five/Six	77.0	78.9	75.7	76.9	77.8	79.0	79.9	85.6	85.5	81.2	72.7
All registered voters	100	100	100	100	100	100	100	100	100	100	100

SOURCE: Adapted from Centraal Bureau voor de Statistiek, *Statistiek der Verkiezingen 1963: Tweede Kamer der Staten-Generaal, 15 mei* (Zeist: De Haan, 1963), pp. 9, 13. Data for 1967 supplied by W. K. J. J. van Ommen Kloeke, Secretary of the Electoral Council, in a letter (dated March 6, 1967) to the author. (The percentages of nonvoters and invalid ballots for 1967 are estimates.)

to consider the minor parties merely as indicators of dissatisfaction and potential instability. They have also played a eufunctional political role in Holland's politics of accommodation. The existence of small parties on the fringes of the four blocs and the absence of significant obstacles to their election to the Second Chamber provide outlets for dissatisfaction; they are the safety valves of the system. The minor parties have ample opportunity to blow off steam in the Chamber. Even when a time limit is put on debate, the splinter groups always receive proportionally more time to speak than the larger parties. But they do not participate directly in the politics of accommodation and do not affect the course of public policy. They are ignored in the formation of new cabinets and left out of all attempts to solve grave crises by summit diplomacy. As long as they remain small, their nuisance potential is low.

At the same time, the popular support they receive serves as a valuable indicator of political dissatisfaction to the leaders of the major parties. It serves to remind the bloc elites that the task of interbloc accommodation should not be pursued at the expense of the equally crucial task of maintaining effective intrabloc understanding. The political climate must be kept cool—and votes for the minor parties constitute a political thermometer. The appearance of minor party strength in provincial and municipal elections performs the same function. For instance, the big parties were jolted in the 1935 provincial elections when the minor parties rolled up a total vote of 20.3 per cent and again in 1966 when the vote was 18 per cent including especially large gains for the Pacifists on the left and the Farmers party on the right.[30]

[30] H. Daalder, "De kleine politieke partijen: Een voorlopige poging tot inventarisatie," *Acta Politica*, Vol. 1, Nos. 1–4 (1965–66), pp. 184, 196. This article is an excellent summary of the small-party phenomenon after 1918. See also J. Niezing, "De kleine partij: Enkele hypothesen," *Sociologische Gids*, Vol. 10, No. 5 (September–October 1963), pp. 264–272.

It would not be difficult for the large established parties to eliminate or drastically curtail the presence of splinter groups in the Second Chamber by changing the electoral law. A return to the single-member constituency system but with plurality elections (as in Britain and the United States) would easily accomplish this. But Geismann's careful investigation of the probable results of such a move shows that it would not only eliminate the splinter parties but also, barring a complete realignment of the party system, gravely affect the Big Five: the Liberal party and the two Protestant parties would be too small to survive under this system, and the Catholic party would be at a disadvantage because of its geographical concentration of strength in the Southern provinces. Only the Labor party would stand to gain.[31]

Relatively small modifications of the proportional representation system could make it more difficult for the minor parties to win election without upsetting the relative strengths of the major parties. Tables 31 and 32 present the hypothetical results of the 1963 and 1967 elections on the assumption that the eighteen electoral districts that are now only used for administrative purposes would be separate districts—instead of the present rule that the entire country is a single electoral area.[32] The seats were first distributed among the districts in proportion to the number of valid ballots cast in

[31] Geismann, *Politische Struktur*, pp. 161–178. The consequences of a two-ballot system (as in the French Fifth Republic) are much harder to predict because of the large number of electoral alignments that would be possible. See also M. R. Mok, "Terug naar het districtenstelsel?" *Socialisme en Democratie*, Vol. 23, No. 4 (April 1966), pp. 246–272.

[32] This kind of speculation always contains dangers. A change of rules would certainly have at least some effect on both parties and voters. To the modifications hypothesized in Tables 31, 32, and 33, the smaller parties might react either by withdrawal or by presenting joint lists, and the voters might either give less support to the smaller parties because they might not want to waste their votes, or, of course, *more* support out of feelings of sympathy with the plight of the splinter parties.

each district, and then proportionally allocated to the parties within each district, both according to the d'Hondt formula. The separate districts rule would have virtually eliminated the small parties in the 1963 elections. Only the Communists and Pacifists would have received a few seats because of their concentrated strength in Amsterdam and the large size of this electoral district. In 1967, when the small parties made impressive gains, all except one would have won entry to the Second Chamber but with considerably smaller delegations: together they would have had only 7—instead of 27—seats.

An alternative rule, requiring a minimum vote of 5 per cent (as in the German Federal Republic), would be much more effective in barring small parties from the Second Chamber. Even in the 1967 election, none of the small parties received this minimum percentage of the total vote, although both the Farmers party and the Democrats '66 came close, and the Chamber would have been the exclusive domain of the Big Five (see Table 33).

The outcome of the 1967 election has caused new interest in such modifications, but they have never received very serious consideration before. Proposals similar to the two hypothetical rules discussed above but less far-reaching—a three per cent rule and the division of the country into four real electoral districts—were discussed in the Second Chamber during the 1930's but did not get anywhere.[33] One reason for the failure to act against the small parties is the appreciation of their useful political function. But more important is the widespread conviction that proportionality is the operational equivalent of justice. And for the elite, proportionality is a basic "rule of the game" in the politics of accommodation.[34] The rule of proportionality in general, including proportional representation as the electoral system, cannot

[33] Oud, *Het jongste verleden*, Vol. 5, pp. 165–166.
[34] See above, pp. 127–129.

TABLE 31. HYPOTHETICAL RESULTS OF THE DISTRICTS RULE IN THE 1963 ELECTION

Electoral district	Catholic	Labor	Liberal	Anti-Revolu-tionary	Chr. Hist. Union	Pacifist Social-ist	Com-mu-nist	Polit-ical Re-formed	Farmers	Re-formed Polit-ical League	Total
Groningen	0	3	1	1	1	0	0	0	0	0	6
Friesland	0	3	0	2	1	0	0	0	0	0	6
Drenthe	0	2	1	1	0	0	0	0	0	0	4
Zwolle	4	4	1	1	1	0	0	0	0	0	11
Arnhem	1	4	1	1	2	0	0	0	0	0	9
Nijmegen	6	2	0	0	0	0	0	0	0	0	8
Utrecht	3	3	1	1	1	0	0	0	0	0	9
Amsterdam	2	5	2	0	0	1	2	0	0	0	12
Den Helder	3	2	1	0	0	0	0	0	0	0	6
Haarlem	3	3	2	1	1	0	0	0	0	0	10

TABLE 31. (*continued*)

Electoral district	Party										
	Catholic	Labor	Liberal	Anti-Revolutionary	Chr. Hist. Union	Pacifist Socialist	Communist	Political Reformed	Farmers	Reformed Political League	Total
Rotterdam	2	6	1	1	0	0	0	0	0	0	10
The Hague	2	4	2	0	0	0	0	0	0	0	8
Leyden	3	2	1	1	1	0	0	0	0	0	8
Dordrecht	2	4	1	2	1	0	0	0	0	0	10
Zealand	1	1	0	0	1	0	0	0	0	0	3
Bois-le-Duc	10	1	0	0	0	0	0	0	0	0	11
Tilburg	7	1	0	0	0	0	0	0	0	0	8
Limburg	10	1	0	0	0	0	0	0	0	0	11
Total	59	51	15	12	10	1	2	0	0	0	150
Actual Results	50	43	16	13	13	4	4	3	3	1	150

SOURCE: Calculated from the figures presented in Centraal Bureau voor de Statistiek, *Statistiek der Verkiezingen* 1963, pp. 26–29.

TABLE 32. HYPOTHETICAL RESULTS OF THE DISTRICTS RULE IN THE 1967 ELECTION

Electoral district	Catholic	Labor	Liberal	Anti-Revolu-tionary	Chr. Hist. Union	Farmers	Demo-crats '66	Com-mu-nist	Paci-fist Social-ist	Polit-ical Re-formed	Re-formed Polit-ical League	Total
Groningen	0	3	1	1	1	0	0	0	0	0	0	6
Friesland	0	3	0	2	1	0	0	0	0	0	0	6
Drenthe	0	2	1	1	0	0	0	0	0	0	0	4
Zwolle	4	3	1	1	2	0	0	0	0	0	0	11
Arnhem	1	3	1	1	2	1	0	0	0	0	0	9
Nijmegen	5	2	0	0	0	1	0	0	0	0	0	8
Utrecht	3	3	1	1	1	0	0	0	0	0	0	9
Amsterdam	2	4	1	1	0	0	1	2	1	0	0	12
Den Helder	3	2	1	1	0	0	0	0	0	0	0	7
Haarlem	3	3	2	1	1	0	0	0	0	0	0	10

TABLE 32. (continued)

Electoral district	Party											
	Catholic	Labor	Liberal	Anti-Revolutionary	Chr. Hist. Union	Farmers	Democrats '66	Communist	Pacifist Socialist	Political Reformed	Reformed Political League	Total
Rotterdam	1	6	1	1	0	0	0	0	0	0	0	9
The Hague	1	3	2	1	0	0	0	0	0	0	0	7
Leyden	3	2	1	1	1	0	0	0	0	0	0	8
Dordrecht	2	4	1	2	1	0	0	0	0	1	0	11
Zealand	1	1	0	0	1	0	0	0	0	0	0	3
Bois-le-Duc	9	1	1	0	0	0	0	0	0	0	0	11
Tilburg	7	1	0	0	0	0	0	0	0	0	0	8
Limburg	10	1	0	0	0	0	0	0	0	0	0	11
Total	55	47	15	15	11	2	1	2	1	1	0	150
Actual Results	42	37	17	15	12	7	7	5	4	3	1	150

SOURCE: Calculated from data supplied by W. K. J. J. van Ommen Kloeke, Secretary of the Electoral Council, in a letter (dated March 6, 1967) to the author.

be changed without affecting the peaceful settlement of 1917. The proportional-representation system is more than just another expedient method of counting votes. This is

TABLE 33.   HYPOTHETICAL RESULTS OF THE 5-PER-CENT RULE
IN THE 1963 AND 1967 ELECTIONS

	1963		1967	
Party	Hypothetical Results	Actual Results	Hypothetical Results	Actual Results
Catholic	55	50	51	42
Labor	48	43	45	37
Liberal	17	16	20	17
Anti- Revolutionary	15	13	19	15
Chr. Hist. Union	15	13	15	12
Farmers	0	3	0	7
Democrats '66	0	0	0	7
Communist	0	4	0	5
Pacifist Socialist	0	4	0	4
Political Reformed	0	3	0	3
Reformed Political League	0	1	0	1
Total seats	150	150	150	150

SOURCE: See Tables 31 and 32.

what foes of proportional representation like Geismann (who states that the "electoral system used in Holland does not contribute anything to a process of political integration"[35]) fail to appreciate.

A strong majority of public opinion supports the reluctance to tamper with the electoral system. In 1954 the fol-

[35] Geismann, p. 149.

lowing question was asked: "There are countries where a party has to get more than one seat in order to enter the Chamber. If the party does not get this [minimum], it receives no seats at all. Do you think this is right or wrong?" The result was 41 to 31 against this rule with 28 per cent undecided. And most of the respondents stuck to their opinions when they were asked a follow-up question urging the view that this obstacle would be helpful in preventing the presence of too many parties in the Chamber. They now favored it but only by a 39–34 margin with 27 per cent undecided.[36]

THE QUALITY OF DEMOCRACY

The cardinal contribution which deferential attitudes make to sustaining the politics of accommodation raises serious questions about the quality of democracy in such an accommodation system. Deference, passivity, and lack of interest are the opposites of the traditional democratic civic virtues. In Chapter IV we argued that Holland is a stable and viable democracy,[37] but how democratic is it really?

The quality of Dutch democracy has been criticized on a number of grounds. Elections are said to be meaningless because the voters are not presented with clear alternatives. Issues are not sharply defined, and responsibility for past governmental policy cannot be plainly determined because of the fuzzy line between government and opposition parties. And even when, occasionally, the voters do happen to get the opportunity to make a real choice, their verdict may be disregarded by the parties of the establishment in the formation of a new cabinet. In the campaign preceding the Second Chamber elections of 1925, for instance, all debates focused

[36] Nederlands Instituut voor de Publieke Opinie, *De Nederlandse kiezer*, pp. 61–62.
[37] See above, pp. 71–77.

on the forceful leader of the Anti-Revolutionary party, H. Colijn. The results were disastrous for Colijn. His own party suffered the heaviest defeat, losing three of its sixteen seats, and the parties that had unequivocally opposed him scored the highest gains. But Colijn became the new prime minister.[38] In 1956, the Labor party and the Catholic party were the main antagonists. Both depicted the contest as one between their top leaders: "Drees or Romme." The Labor party was victorious, winning one more seat than the Catholics. But the two parties patched up their differences and entered the new cabinet together. The voters were asked to choose between the two, but they got "Drees *and* Romme." Similarly, both the 1959 and 1963 elections had shown strong support for the Catholic-Protestant-Liberal coalition. But in 1965 the cabinet was reshuffled—the Labor party came in and the Liberals and the Christian Historical Union were forced out—without any popular mandate.

The powerful Social and Economic Council is not elected and is far removed from popular control. One-third of its members are selected by the cabinet which is in turn dependent on the confidence of the popularly elected Second Chamber. But the other two-thirds are not selected by direct or indirect democratic process. The fifteen workers seats are simply filled by the three large labor unions to which only about a third of all workers belong.[39] On the other hand, the Council certainly does represent the important population groups, and it is, of course, under the ultimate control of parliament which can change or even abolish it.

Especially among liberal intellectuals in Holland one finds considerable criticism of the lack of excitement and transparency in the political system. They resent the secrecy, dullness, and diffuseness of politics, but feel frustrated and

[38] P. J. Oud, *Honderd jaren, 1840–1940: Een eeuw van staatkundige vormgeving in Nederland* (Assen: Van Gorcum, 1954), pp. 272–274.

[39] Geismann, pp. 121–122.

powerless to change it. The bloc leaders exercise a kind of autocratic power within their own spheres, which does tend to set definite limits to individual freedom. There are no formal obstacles to freedom of expression, for instance, but the mass media are a virtual monopoly of the bloc organizations. In Kornhauser's terms, Holland is neither a pluralistic nor a mass society, but a "communal society," characterized by strong intermediate groups that are *inclusive* in the sense that they—or, as in Holland, the closely interconnected set of organizations in each bloc—"encompass all aspects of their members' lives."[40]

All these criticisms are valid. But is it fair to measure the quality of Dutch democracy against the standards of the ideal model? The criticisms are the arguments of democratic perfectionists who fail to perceive that no democracy can survive without political stability, and that stability in a deeply divided society can only be achieved at the expense of deviating to some extent from the ideal democratic norm. As Robert A. Dahl states, "conflicts involving subcultures . . . [are] too explosive to be managed by ordinary parliamentary opposition, bargaining, campaigning, and winning elections."[41] Complete liberty and equality depend on fraternity—a strong consensus and a strong feeling of belonging together in a homogenous setting. When fraternity is lacking, *peaceful coexistence* becomes the next highest objective. It may necessitate some deviations from pure democracy, but, if successful, it represents no mean achievement and must not be belittled. Also, as Eckstein reminds us, *all* democracies must have a "healthy element of authoritarianism" because "a representative government must govern as well

[40] William Kornhauser, *The Politics of Mass Society* (New York: The Free Press of Glencoe, 1959), pp. 83–84. See also Grant McConnell, *Private Power and American Democracy* (New York: Knopf, 1966), esp. chaps. 4, 5.

[41] Robert A. Dahl, "Some Explanations," in Dahl, ed., *Political Oppositions,* p. 358.

as represent—must satisfy two elements which, on the evidence, are not easily reconcilable."[42]

In the final analysis, it is impossible to argue that Holland deviates much from the democratic ideal. Dutch democracy has universal suffrage, majority rule, and justice for all. The people elect their own governors, either directly or indirectly, and they have ample opportunity to show any disaffection. And there are no minorities that are disenfranchised, deprived of their civil liberties, or subject to systematic discrimination.

[42] Harry Eckstein, *A Theory of Stable Democracy*, Research Monograph No. 10 (Princeton, Center for International Studies, Princeton University, 1961), p. 11.

Chapter IX

AMENDMENTS TO
PLURALIST THEORY

In terms of the third pluralist proposition, Dutch politics is in most respects a deviant case. What conclusions can be drawn from this case? What is its relevance to pluralist theory? The usual disclaimer about the conclusions to be drawn from a case study are in order here. A case study may be able to disprove a generalization, but only if the generalization is stated in absolute terms—and most of the general propositions in the social sciences are not universal but probabilistic in nature. A single case study can obviously not be the sole basis for a valid generalization. Case studies have a more modest function. In particular, deviant case analysis can lead to the identification of additional variables and to the refinement of concepts and indicators.[1] It will be

[1] See Patricia L. Kendall and Katherine M. Wolf, "The Analysis of Deviant Cases in Communications Research," in Paul F. Lazarsfeld and Frank Stanton, eds., *Communications Research 1948–49* (New York: Harper and Brothers, 1949), pp. 152–157.

argued here that the Dutch case does not invalidate the basic
pluralist thesis concerning the moderating effect of crosscutting cleavages and cross pressures, but rather suggests a number of amendments to it. It serves to point out the relevance
of additional factors and the necessity of making certain crucial distinctions.

In the first place, there are two ways of formulating the
third pluralist thesis. Positively stated, it argues that crosscutting cleavages are favorable to stable and effective democracy; stated negatively, the argument is that the absence of
crosscutting cleavages leads to instability, ineffectiveness,
and disintegration of the system. *In its negative formulation,
the pluralist thesis can become a self-denying prophecy.* If a
society is divided by sharp mutually reinforcing cleavages
with each segment of the population living in its own separate
world, the dangers of a breakdown of the system are clear—
not only to the social scientist but to any reasonably intelli-
gent observer, including the political decision-makers. As
Dahl points out: "The possibility of violence and civil war
always lurks as a special danger in countries with hostile subcultures; and this danger undoubtedly stimulates a search for
alternative responses."[2] Indeed, the more extreme the condition of cleavage and mutual isolation, the clearer the danger
signals are likely to be perceived. Once the peril is recognized, remedies may be applied.

The peaceful settlement of the major divisive issues by the
Dutch political elite in the 1878–1917 period is an example
of this. The religious-ideological blocs were pitted against
each other on the class issue of extending the franchise and
the religious issue of state aid to private denominational
schools. For a long time the rival parties stood their ground,
and the issues remained unresolved while tensions rose. In
the years after about 1910, the political leaders became

[2] Robert A. Dahl, "Some Explanations," in Dahl, ed., *Political
Oppositions in Western Democracies* (New Haven: Yale University
Press, 1966), p. 358.

fully aware of the dangers and decided to find a solution by accommodating their differences. The prime minister self-consciously compared the religious issue with a "wedge" splitting the nation. The leaders of all major parties instituted summit conferences to forge a settlement. And once an accommodation was reached, the elite again unanimously decided to safeguard it and introduce it into the constitution by manipulating the next parliamentary election and thereby avoiding an expression of popular opinion.[3]

The self-denying character of the third pluralist proposition in the context of Dutch politics has been observed by many scholars, albeit only by implication. For instance, Robert C. Bone attempts to explain the satisfactory operation of the party system in spite of the rigidity of the parties, as follows: "Perhaps the explanation lies in the remarkable and persistent Dutch ability to make a *pragmatic success* from a *theoretical impossibility*—the sheer continued physical existence of the Netherlands itself is proof enough of this."[4] Bone's reference to a "theoretical impossibility" can be stated more accurately as a theoretical improbability which is recognized as such. Dutch political scientist Daalder argues that one reason for the stability and strength of Dutch cabinets is that "they are considered to be pretty well irreplaceable because of what the Dutch have come to call 'difficult party relations'."[5] This seems to be an incongruous explanation: one would expect the troublesome relations among ideological and rigid parties to lead to cabinet instability rather than stability. This conclusion can be reversed only if the self-denying nature of the expectation is added as an explanatory factor. In a different, more general context, Daalder states: "Of crucial importance are not only the severity

[3] See above, pp. 104–112.
[4] Robert C. Bone, "The Dynamics of Dutch Politics," *Journal of Politics*, Vol. 24, No. 1 (February 1962), p. 36 (italics added).
[5] H. Daalder, "Parties and Politics in the Netherlands," *Political Studies*, Vol. 3, No. 1 (February 1955), p. 9.

and incidence of conflicts but also the attitudes political elites take toward the need to solve them by compromise rather than combat." And he calls attention to the fact that "the traumatic memory of past conflicts . . . may either perpetuate conflict, or *cause parties to draw together.*"[6]

The second amendment to the pluralist thesis which the Dutch case suggests, involves two closely related propositions. First, that *overarching cooperation at the elite level can be a substitute for crosscutting affiliations at the mass level.* The four subcultural blocs are closed camps with their own parties, interest groups, media of communication, and so on, but their leaders do bridge the cleavages among the separate camps. They are in continuous contact and communication with each other according to firmly established patterns of cooperation. High-level confederal organs of consultation and accommodation, like the Social and Economic Council where the leaders of all groups with a stake in the economic process meet, provide the institutional means for these crosscutting contacts.[7] Crosscutting cleavages below the elite level may be conducive to stable democracy, but the Dutch case suggests that this is not an essential prerequisite. The much less stringent requirement is the presence of overarching contacts among the elite.

The second proposition is that *when different groups in society have widely divergent interests and values, self-containment and mutual isolation can be more conducive to stable democracy than a high incidence of overlapping affiliations.* This assertion is in accord with the well-established substantive proposition in conflict theory that, in Coser's words, "a conflict is more passionate and more radical when

[6] Hans Daalder, "Parties, Elites, and Political Developments in Western Europe," in Joseph LaPalombara and Myron Weiner, eds., *Political Parties and Political Development* (Princeton: Princeton University Press, 1966), p. 69 (italics added).

[7] See above, pp. 113–115.

it arises out of close relationships."[8] Because passionate and radical conflicts are likely to be detrimental to stable democracy, close relationships between potential rivals can have a harmful, and, conversely, their isolation from each other a salutary, effect on democracy. Quincy Wright argues:

> Ideologies accepted by different groups within a society may be inconsistent without creating tension; but if initiatives or actions are taken by individuals or groups in accord with those inconsistent ideologies, and if these actions lead to contact, tension arises. The degree of intensity of tension tends to increase with decreases in the social distance between the groups and with increases in the amount of energy behind them. If the groups with inconsistent ideologies are in close contact, that is, if the society is closely integrated, the tension will be great.[9]

This argument can also be stated in terms of what Deutsch calls the "transaction-integration balance." He regards transactions of all kinds between people and groups of people as a "burden upon the institutions for peaceful adjustment or change" and asserts that the stability of a political system depends on "its continuing capabilities to produce peaceful adjustments against the growing load of social interaction and potential friction."[10] Therefore, in a society characterized by a very limited political consensus, stability will be enhanced if transactions between ideologically incompatible groups

[8] Lewis A. Coser, *The Functions of Social Conflict* (Glencoe: The Free Press, 1956), p. 71. See also Raymond W. Mack and Richard C. Snyder, "The Analysis of Social Conflict—Toward an Overview and Synthesis," *Journal of Conflict Resolution*, Vol. 1, No. 2 (June 1957), p. 225.

[9] Quincy Wright, "The Nature of Conflict," *Western Political Quarterly*, Vol. 4, No. 2 (June 1951), p. 196.

[10] Karl W. Deutsch, *Political Community at the International Level: Problems of Definition and Measurement* (Garden City, N.Y.: Doubleday, 1954), pp. 39–42.

can be kept to a minimum. The self-containment of such groups and their relative isolation from each other can be a positive value. It is vital to the achievement of peaceful co-existence by methods of accommodation.

This is not an argument in favor of *apartheid*. For one thing, Holland is racially homogeneous and it would be improper to reach any conclusion on racial questions on the basis of the Dutch experience. Secondly, segregation in Holland means self-imposed social isolation, whereas *apartheid* implies the imposition of segregation by a dominant group upon a less favored group. The Dutch case does show, however, that a "separate but equal" doctrine can work. The religious-ideological blocs have fought for and have largely achieved equal status in Dutch society while maintaining their separate identities and their mutual isolation. In other words, social segregation does not necessarily lead to instability nor is it inherently unequal or unjust.

It would be vain to pretend that this conclusion is in agreement with pluralist theory. To the pluralists, any severe discontinuity in patterns of affiliations and allegiances is a danger. The view that mutual isolation always tends to be a serious threat to democracy is clearly represented in Lipset's discussion of the advantages of federalism. He argues that federalism can serve democracy well because it "increases the opportunity for multiple sources of cleavage by adding regional interests and values to the others which crosscut the social structure." But, Lipset says, the boundaries between the federal units should not coincide with the territorial dividing lines between linguistic or religious areas, as in India and Canada: "Democracy needs cleavage within linguistic or religious groups, not between them."[11] The Dutch *confederal* pattern of politics, though it is not geographically a fed-

[11] Seymour Martin Lipset, *Political Man: The Social Bases of Politics* (Garden City, N.Y.: Doubleday, 1960), pp. 91–92.

eral or confederal system, throws doubt on such a categorical conclusion.

The two joint propositions stated above also contain an implicit conclusion regarding the merits of proportional representation and multiparty systems. Lipset maintains that, all other factors being equal, proportional electoral systems and many parties tend to weaken democracy because they diminish crosscutting bases of cleavage.[12] If one accepts the conclusions that in a divided society stable democracy can be achieved by the combination of mutual isolation of the antagonistic segments of the population and overarching elite cooperation, it follows that *proportional representation and a multiparty system can be salutary to democracy because they strengthen the possibilities of accommodation.* In a multiparty system, the parties, representing highly distinct clienteles, tend to be articulative rather than aggregative. But in a divided society like Holland, it is more appropriate for the function of interest aggregation to be performed mainly at the supraparty level—in the cabinet, Social and Economic Council, and parliament.

The explanation of the viability of a democratic system in a plural society in terms of mutual isolation at the rank-and-file level combined with overarching contacts at the elite level is to some extent tautological. The high-level links which cut across the basic social cleavages cannot be considered the cause of viable democracy. The reverse is more true. The pattern of overarching cooperation was established by the elite for the specific purpose of making the system work efficiently. This does not mean a retreat from the proposition that cross-cutting contacts at the elite level can be a substitute for cross-cutting cleavages throughout society. They can indeed serve the same function. But whereas overlapping affiliations at the mass level, if present to high degree in a particular sys-

[12] *Ibid.*, pp. 90–91.

tem, can be regarded as a *cause* of the moderation and pragmatism necessary in a stable democracy, overlapping contacts at the elite level can only be considered a *method* for
maintaining democracy. To find the cause, we have to in-
quire into the factors responsible for the establishment and
maintenance of overarching contacts as an efficient method
of cooperation.

The basic prerequisites for the success of such a system of
political accommodation are a clear recognition by the elite
of the gravity of the problems confronting the system and the
constant peril of disintegrative tendencies—in other words,
the awareness of the fundamental validity of the third pluralist thesis which may turn it into a self-denying prediction—
plus both the willingness and the capability of resolving the
difficulties. There must be a high degree of commitment to
the maintenance of the system and the ability to translate this
commitment into practical results. In short, what is needed
is, to borrow Rothman's term, "prudent leadership."[13]

The example of the Netherlands provides some clues to
the emergence of prudent leadership. One important factor
predisposing the elite to prudent political action is the permanent minority position of *all* blocs. The Catholic bloc,
which is the largest, commands the allegiance of only slightly
more than a third of the population. The blocs are, furthermore, substantially equal in size. No single bloc can dominate the system or realistically expect to achieve majority
status in the foreseeable future. This objective situation is
conducive to a moderate and pragmatic attitude among the
elite. A situation where a dominant majority faces a distinct
but small minority would not give rise to moderation as easily. It is instructive to recall that in Madison's and Rousseau's
treatment of the second type of pluralism, the desirability of
smallness—or minority position—and equality of groups

[13] See above, p. 11.

was emphasized.[14] Dutch politics fits these criteria very well. A parallel at the international level is the multiple balance of power which, all other factors being constant, is more stable than a simple balance of power.

A second set of factors that are conducive to prudent leadership derive from the fact that the basic cleavages in Dutch society—religion and class—do cut across each other at an almost perfectly straight angle. The Catholic and Calvinist blocs are true cross sections of the Dutch people, resembling the class composition of the population as a whole very closely and differing only in religion. Moreover, in these two blocs the religious commitment is sufficiently strong to override class differences to a large extent. For the Catholics, for instance, there is one Catholic party rather than both working-class and middle-class Catholic parties. Still, there are class differences and divergent economic interests in the Catholic bloc, and the heterogeneous class composition of the party requires the reconciliation of these interests within the party. The party leaders are under constant cross pressures from the different wings of the party, which predispose them to moderation and compromises both in intraparty and interparty relations. It is impossible to account for Holland's stable democracy without reference to this crucial political role of the religious parties, particularly the Catholic party.

This conclusion highlights the importance of two of the modifications of the third pluralist proposition discussed in Chapter I. First, overlapping membership should be interpreted broadly as membership not only in associational groups but also in potential and nonassociational groups. The lower-class element of the Catholic bloc is not an organized group. Nor is it a clearly identifiable separate community within the Catholic bloc. But it does constitute a categoric group whose political and economic interests do not

[14] See above, pp. 5–6.

always coincide with the middle-class element of the Catholic bloc. The organized Catholic party, held together by the cohesive force of religion, transcends the class cleavage. Secondly, the cross pressures that lead to moderation are especially significant at the elite level. Here again the Catholic party can serve as the best example: the party leaders must reduce the intensity of their claims in the economic realm because of the heterogeneity of their party's clientele.[15]

On the other hand, the extent of pressures on the elite must not be exaggerated. In Dutch politics, the elites have usually enjoyed great freedom to act independently without constant demands from their followers—a freedom vital to the success of the system of overarching cooperation among the blocs. Pressures from below do exist, but more as potential pressures which constitute part of the total political context for the elite, than as constantly active demands keeping the bloc leaders on the defensive. There are limits on the elite's freedom of action but they are not constrictive.

The high degree of organization in Dutch society promotes this wide latitude for the bloc leaders. Dutch society is highly pluralistic in the sense of the second pluralist proposition. Many organized groups are active in all spheres of social and political life, and the percentage of individual affiliation with these organizations is high. Such groups constitute buffers between the elite and the mass. They offer to the rank and file an effective avenue for achieving redress of grievances; at the same time, they provide the leaders with sufficient freedom from encroachment by the rank and file, and, consequently, the necessary latitude for the process of political accommodation with the leaders of other blocs. This is especially true in Holland because oligarchical control, to which all organizations have a strong tendency as Michels points out, has been developed to an extraordinary degree of perfection. For the parties the list system of proportional

15 See above, pp. 88–93, 118–119.

representation has been an additional factor behind firm elite domination. It should be noted that the highly organized and oligarchical character of Dutch society which supports a stable democracy (of the accommodation type), confirms the essential validity of the second pluralist proposition: *A multiplicity of associations and a high degree of affiliation can be conducive to democracy even when there is very little overlapping membership across basic social cleavages.*

The acquiescence by the rank and file in their leaders' oligarchical power requires a highly deferential attitude. And deference has long been bountifully available in the Netherlands. The commitment to system maintenance and prudent leadership complemented by deference, are crucial to the success of the accommodation approach to stable democracy. These three factors are all subjective in nature. Some objective conditions of the social structure, like the multiple balance of power, are helpful in preserving these subjective orientations, but they cannot fully explain them. They might be explained in terms of enduring traits in the Dutch national character. The three vital subjective orientations have a long history and antedate the rise of democracy by many centuries. The will to preserve the system is closely related to Dutch nationalism and national symbols; deference and obedience are emphasized both in Calvinist and Roman Catholic doctrine; and the habits of pragmatism and prudence in politics—which in Holland is the "business" of politics, not a "game" of politics—can be traced back to Holland's history as a merchant nation.

However, national character analysis is more of a hindrance than a help. It obscures the fact that the Dutch are by no means unique in exhibiting these subjective qualities, and that the subjective minimum requirements for the politics of accommodation are not unusually difficult demands. It is not necessary to resort to Bentley's and Truman's conclusion that a strong common "habit background" is a precondition for democracy in either a society characterized by crosscutting cleavages or one with mutually reinforcing cleavages and the process of accommodation.[16] The political consensus does not have to be comprehensive and strong. It must include, as a minimum, the commitment to maintain the system, reinforced by habits of prudence and deference, but it does not have to include the traditional democratic civic virtues.

The whole set of attitudes epitomized as "deference"—including respect, obedience, apathy, passivity, and acquiescence—are almost universal characteristics of mass political cultures, as noted by many writers. As Jack L. Walker points out, especially the prevalent elitist theory of democracy is founded on the empirical "fact of political life" that widespread apathy is the rule rather than the exception; it is "something to be anticipated, a prerequisite for democratic stability."[17] Almond and Verba describe the civic culture as a "balanced political culture in which political activity, involvement, and rationality exist but are balanced by passivity, traditionality, and commitment to parochial values." They conclude on the basis of their comparative empirical analysis that both the American and British political cultures approximate this ideal. In the United States they find a high development of the participant role but also a persistence of "the more passive roles of subject and parochial." The British are said to have a "deferential civic culture," which also approximates the ideal but in which "the deferential subject role is more strongly developed and widespread." And they find that deferential attitudes are even stronger in Germany: "Awareness of politics and political activity, though substantial, tend to be passive and formal.

[16] See above, pp. 13–14.
[17] Jack L. Walker, "A Critique of the Elitist Theory of Democracy," *American Political Science Review*, Vol. 60, No. 2 (June 1966), p. 291.

... And norms favoring active political participation are not well developed."[18]

Michels writes that the masses are both politically incompetent and uninterested: "Among the citizens who enjoy political rights the number of those who have a lively interest in public affairs is insignificant." Furthermore, they have "an immense need for direction and guidance ... accompanied by a genuine cult for the leaders, who are regarded as heroes," and before whom the masses "experience a profound need to prostrate themselves."[19] The authors of the Elmira voting study also conclude that "for large numbers of people motivation [for participation in political life] is weak if not almost absent,"[20] and Dahl points out that, for the ordinary man, "the chances are very great that political activity will always seem rather remote from the main focus of life," and that he "is not, by nature, a political animal."[21]

Many questions remain, of course. What is the exact relationship among the components of the whole set of political orientations referred to as deference? Where is the boundary between deferential attitudes that sustain democratic stability and authoritarian servility that undermines democracy? And what are the exact differences in the incidence of deferential and apathetic attitudes both among different political cultures and within a particular political culture among separate subcultures? The evidence presented in Chapter VIII suggests

[18] Gabriel A. Almond and Sidney Verba, *The Civic Culture: Political Attitudes and Democracy in Five Nations* (Princeton: Princeton University Press, 1963), pp. 31–32, 428–429, 440–441, 455–456.

[19] Robert Michels, *Political Parties: A Sociological Study of the Oligarchical Tendencies of Modern Democracy*, trans. Eden and Cedar Paul (Glencoe: The Free Press, 1958), pp. 54, 58, 73.

[20] Bernard R. Berelson, Paul F. Lazarsfeld, and William N. McPhee, *Voting: A Study of Opinion Formation in a Presidential Campaign* (Chicago: University of Chicago Press, 1954), p. 308.

[21] Robert A. Dahl, *Who Governs? Democracy and Power in an American City* (New Haven: Yale University Press, 1961), pp. 224–225.

that deference is especially strong in Holland compared with
other countries.[22] To the extent that the politics of accommodation depends on a high degree of deference, Dutch political culture provides an especially suitable environment. But
it does not necessarily follow that the politics of accommodation would be unworkable where deference is somewhat
less prominent. Furthermore, the second subjective requisite
for the politics of accommodation—commitment to system
maintenance—is also by no means a unique quality. Chapter
V showed that this commitment is present in the Netherlands, but that it is not particularly strong—probably much
less so than elsewhere.[23] It is reasonable to assume that a
stronger commitment to system maintenance may be able to
make up for a comparatively weaker deferential orientation.

These subjective qualities are prerequisites for the politics
of accommodation, but they are not extraordinary phenomena. This means that we do not have to abandon pluralist
theory in favor of national character analysis in order to explain the politics of accommodation. All that is necessary is
to amend pluralist theory, primarily by taking into account
the self-denying character of the third pluralist proposition
and the possibility of crosscutting links at the elite level.
These are also the crucial ingredients of the third subjective
prerequisite: prudent leadership. Therefore, *the politics of
accommodation fits perfectly within the context of pluralist
theory (thus amended) as a genuinely alternative model to
the model of pluralistic democracy based on crosscutting
cleavages.* The United States and Great Britain approximate
the pluralistic model and Holland approximates the accommodation model. But Holland is not the only example; postwar Austria comes to mind as another and possibly even
better example. Here the experience of political turmoil during the First Republic served as a lesson in the essential valid-

[22] See above, pp. 144–162.
[23] See above, pp. 78–88.

ity of the third pluralist proposition. Once the leaders of the rival Catholic and Socialist blocs had learned the lesson, it became a self-denying proposition. From then on, until the Catholic electoral victory in early 1966, the Second Republic was run after the pattern of accommodation. A Catholic-Socialist grand coalition, based on formal coalition pacts, ruled the country. The coalition committee became the most important overarching organ of accommodation, and pro-portionality *(Proporz)* became the outstanding rule of the game.[24]

The viability of a democratic system must not be evaluated solely against the criteria of pluralistic democracy. The accommodation model provides not only an alternative model, but one for which the social prerequisites are considerably lower. Deep, mutually reinforcing social cleavages do not form an insuperable obstacle to viable democracy. The crucial factor in the establishment and preservation of democratic norms and democratic stability is the quality of leadership. The politics of accommodation opens up the possibility of viable democracy even where the social conditions appear unpromising. For those committed to the democratic creed, this is an optimistic and happy conclusion.

[24] See Alexander Vodopivec, *Wer regiert in Österreich?* (Vienna: Verlag für Geschichte und Politik, 1962); Herbert P. Secher, "Coalition Government: The Case of the Second Austrian Republic," *American Political Science Review*, Vol. 52, No. 3 (September 1958), pp. 791–808; Uwe Kitzinger, *Britain, Europe and Beyond: Essays in European Politics* (Leyden: Sijthoff 1964), pp. 84–106; Frederick C. Engelmann, "Haggling for the Equilibrium: The Renegotiation of the Austrian Coalition, 1959," *American Political Science Review*, Vol. 56, No. 3 (September 1962), pp. 651–62; and Engelmann, "Austria: The Pooling of Opposition," in Dahl, ed., *Political Oppositions*, pp. 260–283.

Chapter X
THE BREAKDOWN
OF THE POLITICS
OF ACCOMMODATION

The foundation for the politics of accommodation was laid by the peaceful settlement of 1917, and it grew gradually from then on. The rule of proportional distribution of government subsidies enabled the bloc organizations to translate social cleavages into institutional boundaries and to achieve nearly exclusive control within their own spheres. At the same time, the cooperation among the bloc leaders was perfected by the admission of the Socialists to the cabinet in 1939 and by the establishment of the Foundation of Labor in 1945 and of the Social and Economic Council in 1950. The system of accommodation reached its heyday in the 1950's but declined rapidly in the following decade. By the late 1960's, it had broken down completely. The Second Chamber elections of 1967 marked the turning point, and this year can therefore be regarded as the end of half a century of accommodation politics.

CHALLENGES TO BLOC COHESION
AND ELITE RULE

The essential elements of the politics of accommodation are the division of society into a number of distinct and self-contained segments or blocs, overarching cooperation at the elite level, strong deference to the bloc leaders, and, as a result, a high degree of political stability. In all four respects, far-reaching changes have taken place in the 1960's and early 1970's. First of all, the social cleavages between the blocs have lost their sharpness as well as much of their political salience. As a consequence, the special ties between the bloc organizations within each bloc have weakened, and there have been significant attempts to join forces across the cleavages. For instance, a merger between the Socialist and Catholic labor union federations is being prepared. And there is growing cooperation between the Catholic and the two main Protestant parties; in the provincial and local elections of 1970 and 1974, these parties presented joint lists in many places, and a merger at the national level is under serious consideration. Already in 1966, most of the supporters of the religious parties were in favor of such a move.[1]

The decreasing isolation and self-containment of the blocs also manifests itself in the declining allegiance given to the bloc organizations. This applies not only to the major parties (which will be examined in greater detail below)[2] but also to the interest groups and most notably to the media of communication. Neutral newspapers are enjoying enormous gains in circulation. This trend is even more significant in

[1] "Politiek in Nederland: 2," *Revu* (December 24, 1966), p. 34. See also L. P. J. de Bruyn, "Verzuiling en politieke deconfessionalisering," *Acta Politica*, Vol. 7, No. 1 (January 1972), pp. 45–46.

[2] See pp. 201–208.

the area of radio and television. The A.V.R.O., which has always been neutral rather than liberal, became by far the largest of the radio and television associations by joining forces in 1967 with the weekly magazine *Televizier*, which was a neutral and purely commercial competitor for the weekly bulletins that contained articles and program listings of the five established associations. Moreover, a new determinedly neutral organization (T.R.O.S.), which grew out of the ill-fated attempt to set up a North Sea television station, established itself quickly and acquired a sufficiently large membership to put it on a par with the four other large associations.

Among the Dutch Catholics, formerly the most cohesive of the blocs, these changes have occurred at an especially rapid pace. In 1954 the bishops could still issue an injunction, applicable to all Catholics, against membership in the Socialist labor union as well as against regular attention to Socialist newspapers and radio programs and regular attendance at Socialist meetings.[3] In 1965, eleven years later, the bishops issued a statement noting an improvement in the Socialist labor union's attitude toward church and religion and lifting the prohibition against membership in the union. The other injunctions remained in effect, and the bishops also again urged all Catholics to join their own Catholic organizations. But these instructions, too, were soon forgotten as an increasingly liberal spirit pervaded the church.

A second deviation from the essential features of the politics of accommodation has been the rejection by many leaders, mainly on the left of the political spectrum, of overarching cooperation and the "rules of the game." For instance, the 1969 congress of the Labor party adopted a resolution which virtually ruled out any cabinet coalition with the Catholic party. An even more important challenge to the tradition of cooperation and compromise among all of the elites was the "shadow cabinet" formed by the left-

[3] See above, pp. 35–36, 39, 41.

wing parties to oppose the incumbent cabinet in the Second Chamber elections in the spring of 1971 and the fall of 1972. This entailed a serious violation of several rules of the game. Its objective was to draw a sharp line between government parties and opposition parties, to accentuate political differences rather than to depoliticize them, to offer clearcut alternatives rather than to search for compromises in secret negotiations, and to downgrade the rules of concurrent majority and proportional participation in decision making. Similarly, the left-wing parties are also trying to change the tradition of proportionally composed executive organs at the provincial and municipal level into the new rule that all of the executive positions should be occupied by the parties that gain an electoral majority. Finally, a rule that has been widely violated in recent years is the government's right to govern. The Second Chamber has made increasing use of its formal powers to challenge the cabinet. A comparison of the parliamentary session of 1956–1957, during the heyday of the politics of accommodation, with the 1971–1972 session reveals the following changes: The number of amendments that were introduced rose from 109 to 309, the number of motions from 20 to 176, the number of interpellations from 5 to 19, and the number of questions from 211 to 2,092. Furthermore, the Second Chamber adopted the new political weapon of hearings in 1968.[4]

Third, deference and indifference are on the wane. The turnout in the Second Chamber elections of 1971 and 1972 was quite high—79.1 per cent and 83.5 per cent, respectively —in spite of the abolition of compulsory voting in 1970 and in spite of the fact that in the 1972 elections the 18 to 21 year age group, which is generally not highly motivated to vote, could participate for the first time. There has also been a steady increase in preferential votes, indicating a

[4] M. P. C. M. van Schendelen, "Groei en achtergronden van parlementair aktivisme," *Beleid en Maatschappij*, Vol. 1, No. 4 (April 1974), p. 114.

growing voter independence: from 3.4 per cent of the total
vote in 1956 to 11.7 per cent in 1972.[5] Public opinion polls
show consistently high support for a series of democratic
reforms that have been debated in Holland in recent years.
The majority in a 1972 survey in favor of a prime minister
directly elected by the voters was 60 to 29 per cent; the
majority favoring an elected mayor was a similarly high 61 to
31 per cent; and the majority in favor of instituting a referendum was an even more impressive 61 to 22 per cent.
When asked what a member of the Second Chamber should
do in the case of a conflict between his own and his party
supporters' opinion, the respondents said that he should
behave like a delegate of his voters (62 per cent) rather than
a Burkean representative (27 per cent).[6]

A more conspicuous manifestation of growing political
activism is the proliferation of ad hoc promotional groups
that are generally small, temporary, and without formal
organization and that usually try to exert pressure by un-
orthodox methods outside the established institutional chan-
nels. These methods include acts of civil disobedience, which
are sometimes motivated by genuinely altruistic ideals—for
instance, the occupation of embassies and consulates to protest perceived injustices in foreign countries or the blockading
of roads to protest pollution or traffic hazards. Sometimes,

5 Centraal Bureau voor de Statistiek, *Statistiek der Verkiezingen
1956: Tweede Kamer der Staten-Generaal, 13 juni* (Zeist: De Haan,
1957), p. 71; Centraal Bureau voor de Statistiek, *Statistiek der
Verkiezingen 1972: Tweede Kamer der Staten-Generaal, 29 november* (The Hague: Staatsuitgeverij, 1973), pp. 22, 132.
6 Werkgroep nationaal verkiezingsonderzoek 1972, *De Nederlandse kiezer '72* (Alphen aan den Rijn: Samsom, 1973), pp. 93, 95–
96. One bit of contrary evidence should also be mentioned. In 1954,
10 per cent of the respondents said that they were very much interested in politics, 40 per cent were fairly interested, and 47 per cent
were not interested. The percentages in the surveys of 1967, 1971,
and 1972 turned out to be virtually identical. See H. Daalder,
Politisering en lijdelijkheid in de Nederlandse politiek (Assen: Van
Gorcum, 1974), p. 71.

however, they are used for plain self-interest by groups such as university students, increasingly clamorous since their May 1969 mini-revolution, who demand lower tuition fees; workers occupying factories to prevent them from being closed; and gas station owners who flouted the government's rationing decrees in early 1974.

Fourth, there have been many unmistakable signs of political instability in recent years. The frequent resort to civil disobedience may itself be regarded as such a sign. Overt violence has been rare, except in the two serious disturbances in Amsterdam in 1966 caused by Princess Beatrix's marriage to a German who had served in Hitler's army and by wage claims of nonunionized construction workers. Cabinet stability, measured in terms of the gross indicators used earlier,[7] has also declined. In the twenty years between 1945 and 1965 there were five prime ministers presiding over nine different cabinets; in the nine years since 1965 there have been the same number of prime ministers and six cabinets. The formation of the Den Uyl cabinet following the Second Chamber elections of November 1972 broke all previous records when it lasted more than five months (164 days). Moreover, this inordinate length of time was used less for serious bargaining than for efforts to overcome the stubborn unwillingness of the eventual coalition partners to start negotiations.

CHANGES IN THE PARTY SYSTEM

The revolutionary nature of the changes in Dutch politics is shown most clearly by the convulsions of the party system. While the politics of accommodation reigned supreme, the large parties were the organized political manifestations of the four blocs, party preference and bloc membership virtually coincided, and party support was very stable.[8] This is no longer true as the blocs have lost their

[7] See above, pp. 75–76.
[8] See above, pp. 25–26, 34–35.

cohesive and exclusive character. Table 34 shows the electoral strengths of the parties in the postwar Second Chamber elections. Because of the stability of party support until the 1960's, the results of the five elections from 1946 to 1959 have been averaged. Only the fourteen parties that won Second Chamber seats in 1972 are listed separately in the table. Four aspects of the changing party system deserve special attention.

In the first place, the support for the Big Five of the parties that used to be the joint managers of the politics of accommodation has declined drastically. In Chapter VIII, the combined strength of the Big Five was measured in terms of the percentage of the total electorate that voted for these parties, on the assumption that the votes for the minor parties, the invalid ballots, and the unused ballots of the nonvoters could be interpreted as anti-system or anti-establishment votes.[9] Because of the abolition of compulsory voting in 1970, this measure no longer yields comparable results. However, the combined vote for the Big Five as a percentage of the total valid vote also gives a clear picture of recent trends. As Table 34 shows, the Big Five declined from an average of 88.6 per cent in the 1946–1959 elections to a low of 71.9 per cent in 1971, which increased again, but only slightly, to 73.0 per cent in 1972.

The second important trend is the change in the relative strengths of the individual Big Five parties. The losses have been suffered mainly by the three religious parties whereas the two secular parties have maintained themselves quite well. The Labor party reached a nadir of 23.5 per cent in 1967 but has succeeded in climbing back to 27.3 per cent in 1972—only about two percentage points below their average in 1946–1959. The Liberals have actually registered substantial gains; their 14.4 per cent of the 1972 vote represents more than a 60 per cent increase over the early postwar average. Among the religious parties, the Anti-Revolution-

[9] See above, pp. 167–168.

TABLE 34. SECOND CHAMBER ELECTIONS,
1946–1959, 1963, 1967, 1971 AND 1972
(In per cent of the valid vote)

Party	1946–1959	1963	1967	1971	1972
Catholic	30.8	31.9	26.5	21.9	17.7 —
Labor	29.2	28.0	23.5	24.7	27.3
Liberal	8.8	10.3	10.7	10.4	14.4
Anti-Revolutionary	11.3	8.7	9.9	8.6	8.8 —
Chr. Hist. Union	8.5	8.6	8.1	6.3	4.8 —
Communist	6.3	2.8	3.6	3.9	4.5
Political Reformed	2.3	2.3	2.0	2.3	2.2
Ref. Pol. League	0.4	0.8	0.9	1.6	1.8
Pacifist Socialist	0.4	3.0	2.9	1.4	1.5
Farmers	0.1	2.1	4.7	1.1	1.9
Democrats '66	–	–	4.5	6.8	4.2
Dem. Socialists '70	–	–	–	5.3	4.1
Radical	–	–	–	1.8	4.8
Roman Catholic	–	–	–	–	0.9
Other	1.9	1.5	2.7	3.9	1.1
Big Five	88.6	87.5	78.7	71.9	73.0
Old splinter parties	9.4	8.9	9.4	9.2	10.0
New splinter parties	0.1	2.1	9.2	15.0	15.9

NOTE: Three parties participated in some but not all of the five elections from 1946 to 1959: The Pacifist Socialists and the Farmers party participated only in 1959 and won 1.8 and 0.7 per cent of the vote, respectively; the Reformed Political League participated only in 1952 (winning 0.7 per cent of the vote), in 1956 (0.6 per cent), and in 1959 (0.7 per cent).

SOURCE: Adapted from Centraal Bureau voor de Statistiek, *Statistiek der verkiezingen 1972: Tweede Kamer der Staten-Generaal, 29 november* (The Hague: Staatsuitgeverij, 1973), p. 23.

aries have not lost as much as the others; their 8.8 per cent in 1972 was even a slight improvement over 1971 but still entailed a loss of more than 20 per cent of the average vote they collected in the first five postwar elections. The really big losers have been the Catholic party and the Christian Historical Union; the fact that they received only 17.7 and 4.8 per cent of the 1972 vote means that they both lost more than 40 per cent of their average support in the 1946–1959 elections. One explanation is the decline in church membership—in the 1971 census 22.5 per cent of the people, compared with 18.4 per cent in 1960, did not belong to a church[10] —as well as decreasing church attendance. But as Table 35 shows, even among Catholics and Reformed Church members who regularly go to church and who used to be the mainstays of the Catholic and Anti-Revolutionary parties, there has been a precipitous drop in party loyalty. The weakness of the Catholic party is especially significant because as the largest center party and, consequently, as the governing party par excellence, it used to have a pivotal position in the politics of accommodation.[11]

 Third, in analyzing the growth of the minor parties, it is essential to distinguish the old ones, described in Chapter VIII,[12] which neatly fit the bloc pattern and have represented the extreme wings of the blocs—the Communists, Pacifists, and the two fundamentalist Protestant splinter parties— from the small parties that have emerged more recently. The share of the vote received by the old splinter parties has been very steady in recent years: generally between 9 and 10 per cent. The big gains were scored by the new splinters— the Farmers, Democrats '66, Radicals, Democratic Socialists '70, and the Roman Catholic party. In 1959 only the Farmers party was in existence and won an almost negligible 0.7

---

[10] Centraal Bureau voor de Statistiek, *Statistisch zakboek '73* (The Hague: Staatsuitgeverij, 1973), p. 60. See also above, p. 16.

[11] See above, pp. 118–121.

[12] See above, pp. 164–167.

TABLE 35. RELIGION AND SUPPORT FOR THE
RELIGIOUS PARTIES, 1956–1972

(In per cent)

Percentage of:	1956	1967	1971	1972
Catholics (regular) for Catholic party	95	77	70	53
Catholics (irregular) for Catholic party	50	37	25	25
Reformed (regular) for Anti-Rev. party	90	88	67	61
Reformed (irregular) for Anti-Rev. party	62	58	40	36
Dutch Ref. (regular) for Chr. Hist. Union	45	54	50	44
Dutch Ref. (irregular) for Chr. Hist. Union	19	14	11	8

SOURCE: Adapted from Arend Lijphart, "The Netherlands: Continuity and Change in Voting Behavior," in Richard Rose, ed., *Electoral Behavior: A Comparative Handbook* (New York: Free Press, 1974), p. 247 (data for 1956); Werkgroep nationaal verkiezingsonderzoek 1972, *De Nederlandse kiezer '72* (Alphen aan den Rijn: Samsom, 1973), p. 32 (data for 1967–1972). Used by permission.

per cent of the vote, compared with a combined vote for the five new parties of 15.9 per cent in 1972.

The common feature of these parties is their youth and also, especially in the case of the Radicals and Democrats '66, their appeal to young voters; but they are not at all alike in other respects. The Farmers party can be characterized as a protest party of the Poujadist variety. Democrats '66 are an explicit anti-accommodation party who favor a thorough realignment of the Dutch party system on pragmatic bases instead of on the old bloc lines. The most distinctive part of their program is democratic reform: the direct popular election of prime ministers and mayors, referenda, and a change in the electoral system in order to assure greater responsiveness by the legislators to their constituents. On the basis of this reformist program, they should be classified as a party of the moderate secular left although at the time of their greatest popular strength, their supporters were more like those of the Liberals than those of Labor in social composition.[13] In 1971, they made a definite turn to the left by joining the Labor and Radical parties in an electoral alliance and in setting up a "shadow cabinet." The Radicals began as a left-wing offshoot of the Catholic party, but they deemphasized the religious character of the new party that they founded in 1968. In 1970 they were joined by dissident left-wing Anti-Revolutionaries, who brought back the element of religious enthusiasm. The Democratic Socialists '70 seceded from the Labor party in 1970 primarily because they opposed the influence of the New Left in the party. Finally, the Roman Catholic party (not to be confused with the much larger Catholic party) is a fundamentalist right-wing group that is opposed to the liberalization of the Dutch Catholic Church.

The political significance of the new splinter parties lies

[13] Arend Lijphart, "The Netherlands: Continuity and Change in Voting Behavior," in Richard Rose, ed., *Electoral Behavior: A Comparative Handbook* (New York: Free Press, 1974), pp. 257–259.

not only in their combined rapid growth in voter support but also in the volatility of the support for the individual parties. Every election since 1963 has produced a bright new star in the party constellation: the Farmers in 1963, Democrats '66 in 1967, Democratic Socialists '70 in 1971, and Radicals in 1972. But most of them have turned out to be falling stars; the Democrats '66 actually reached a high of 12 to 13 per cent support in the opinion polls between 1967 and 1971, but they were virtually wiped out in the 1974 provincial elections—a fate shared by the Democratic Socialists '70. Even more significant is the fact that three of the new splinters were brought into the government very soon after they were founded. The Democratic Socialists joined the Biesheuvel cabinet in 1971, and the Radicals and Democrats '66 joined the cabinet of Socialist prime minister J. M. den Uyl in 1973 after they had already been partners in the "shadow cabinets" of 1971 and 1972.

The fourth and probably most important change in the Dutch party system is that the Labor party, under the increasing influence of the New Left within its own ranks, has essentially become an anti-accommodation party. The New Left has been responsible for reemphasizing such traditional socialist demands as greater economic equality, but it has also been a neo-democratic movement like the Democrats '66—although with more emphasis on participatory democracy than on the more conventional democratic reforms. The new orientation of the Labor party means that the contrast between the Big Five and the minor parties has lost its relevance. The position among the Big Five vacated by Labor was temporarily filled by the pro-accommodation Democratic Socialists '70. The new Five were the parties that formed the cabinet under Anti-Revolutionary prime minister B. W. Biesheuvel in 1971. Together they had 52.5 per cent of the vote and 82 of the 150 Second Chamber seats. After the collapse of the cabinet in 1972 and the subsequent new elections, they only had 49.8 per cent of the vote and the narrowest possible majority of seats: 76 out of 150. They could have, therefore, formed a new cabinet, but the Catholics and Anti-Revolutionaries opted for a swing to the left. After many months of wrangling with the "shadow cabinet" parties, which collected 36.3 per cent of the vote, this resulted in an uneasy five-party coalition with a highly ambivalent attitude toward the politics of accommodation.

THE SECOND DUTCH PARADOX

The first paradox that this book has sought to explain is the stability of Dutch democracy in the 1917–1967 period in spite of the deep, mutually reinforcing social cleavages. The developments since 1967 present a second paradox: Why has Dutch politics become less stable when the cleavages are fading and cross-cutting and overlap are increasing?

This paradox can be stated in terms of a typology based on Gabriel A. Almond's classification of political cultures discussed in Chapter I and the two alternative models of stable democracy—the pluralistic model exemplified by Great Britain and the United States, and the Dutch or Austrian accommodation model—outlined in Chapter IX.[14] Almond distinguishes between the Anglo-American homogeneous political cultures and the Continental European fragmented cultures. The latter are divided into political subcultures—corresponding to the concept of "blocs" as used in this study. Only homogeneous political cultures, Almond argues, can sustain stable democracy. The Dutch example shows, however, that there are two types of stable democracy: one based on a homogeneous culture and one in a fragmented culture but with elite cooperation. The combination of the

[14] See above, pp. 9–10, 194–195. This typology is also used in Lijphart, "Typologies of Democratic Systems," *Comparative Political Studies*, Vol. 1, No. 1 (April 1968), esp. pp. 35–39; and Lijphart, "Kentering in de Nederlandse politiek," *Acta Politica*, Vol. 4, No. 3 (April 1969), pp. 231–247.

two dimensions of political culture and elite behavior lead to the fourfold typology of democratic regimes of Figure 1. The centrifugal type of democracy tends to be unstable; examples are the Third and Fourth French Republics, Weimar Germany, and postwar Italy. The centripetal (pluralistic) and consociational (accommodation) types can sustain stable democracy. And the depoliticized type appears prima facie to be the most stable. In recent years, Dutch politics, with its tradition of elite cooperation and its less and less divided political culture, has been moving from the consocia-

FIGURE 1. TYPOLOGY OF DEMOCRATIC REGIMES

POLITICAL CULTURE

	Homogeneous	Fragmented
Coalescent	Depoliticized Democracy ~~most~~ stable (?)	Consociational Democracy (Accommodation Model) ← Dutch
Competitive	Centripetal Democracy (Pluralistic Model) stable	Centrifugal Democracy unstable 3rd & 4th Rep. Weimar Ger.

ELITE BEHAVIOR

tional to the depoliticized type of democracy. Why has this process undermined the stability of Dutch politics? A closer analysis of the typology yields five explanations.

First, the movement toward a more homogeneous political ①

culture has not been a smooth one because it is a multidi-
mensional process in which the movements along the different dimensions have not occurred at a uniform pace. The
erosion of the religious cleavages is much more rapid than
that of the class and ideological cleavages. This uneven
development has made the latter divisions comparatively
more salient, especially among Catholics and Calvinists.
Moreover, the Catholic bloc is merging much faster into a
homogeneous political culture than the Calvinist bloc. For
instance, the Catholic and Socialist labor union federations
seem ready to merge, but their Protestant counterpart stands
aloof. And whereas the Catholic universities have opened
their doors to many non-Catholic professors, the Calvinist
Free University still requires a pledge of allegiance from
its teaching staff. Another uneven development is that the
increasing liberalism within the Catholic and Calvinist blocs
does not equally affect all elements of the blocs. Among
the Calvinists this has resulted, for example, in the establishment of the fundamentalist Evangelical radio and television
association (E.O.), which has become the seventh association of this kind with a relatively small membership comparable with that of the V.P.R.O. The tension between
progressive and conservative elements in the Catholic camp
has been accentuated by the overt support given to the conservatives by the Vatican, as shown by the appointment of
two conservative bishops in defiance of the wishes of the
other Dutch bishops.

These uneven developments also explain several of the
changes in the Dutch party system—which are not in accord with Otto Kirchheimer's prediction that the increasingly
homogeneous political cultures of the Western countries
would lead to the growth of large, unideological "catch-all"
parties.[15] In fact, the fissiparous tendencies in the Dutch party

---

[15] Otto Kirchheimer, "The Transformation of the Western European Party Systems," in Joseph LaPalombara and Myron Weiner,
eds., *Political Parties and Political Development* (Princeton: Prince-

system have been much stronger than the integrative ones. The new salience of class and ideology has weakened the center and has increased the distance between the Liberals on the right and the Socialists on the left; the Democratic Socialists '70 emerged as a reaction to this polarization. It has also caused the secession of the Radicals from the religious parties whereas the religious cleavage is still sufficiently relevant for the Radicals to continue as a separate party instead of merging with Labor; a recent astute analysis of the crisis in Dutch politics characterizes the Radicals as a "new church [with] a strong missionary urge."[16] The lessening of religious differences has made the movement toward a single Catholic-Protestant party possible, but the left-right division now bedevils this effort as the Christian Historical Union has split with its two partners on the issue of joining the left-wing Den Uyl cabinet. The faster disintegration of the Catholic bloc compared with the Calvinists is reflected in the disastrous losses of the Catholic party and the relatively strong position of the Anti-Revolutionaries. Finally, the uneven development within the two religious blocs has resulted in the loss of votes not only to the secular parties and the Radicals but also to the religiously conservative Roman Catholic party and Reformed Political League; the latter used to draw its support exclusively from a small fundamentalist denomination, but it has more than doubled its strength in recent years with the aid of other Protestant voters (see Table 34).

The second explanation is based on the nature of de-politicized democracy. In the typology it appears to be the most stable type, but it bears a strong resemblance to what Robert A. Dahl calls the "democratic Leviathan" of the

---

ton University Press, 1966), pp. 184–200. For a thorough critique of the Kirchheimer thesis in the context of Dutch party developments, see Steven B. Wolinetz, *Party Re-Alignment in the Netherlands* (doctoral dissertation, Yale University, 1973), chaps. 1 and 7.

[16] J. Th. J. van den Berg and H. A. A. Molleman, *Crisis in de Nederlandse politiek* (Alphen aan den Rijn: Samsom, 1974), p. 94.

highly industrialized Western countries, which is "addicted to bargaining and compromise" and "an instrument of political elites." Dahl warned that "there are already faint signs . . . that many young people, intellectuals, and academics reject the democratic Leviathan—not because it is democratic but because, in their view, it is not democratic enough."[17] This normative criticism is, therefore, an inherent source of instability in depoliticized democracies. It is striking that in the same year in which Dahl discerned "faint signs" of neo-democratic opposition—in 1966—the New Left and Democrats '66 appeared on the Dutch political scene as vigorous exponents of the neo-democratic ideology. The reason why this opposition emerged earlier and grew stronger in Holland than elsewhere is that the foundation for it had already been laid during the period of the politics of accommodation, which can be faulted—and, as indicated in Chapter VIII, was in fact often criticized—on the very same grounds as the democratic Leviathan.[18] Furthermore, in comparison with other consociational democracies, the politics of accommodation in Holland had a very long life—unlike in Austria where it lasted only two decades and gave way in 1966 to a more competitive pattern of government—and offered extremely little opportunity for citizen participation in politics —unlike consociational Switzerland with its referenda and other instruments of direct democracy.

The third explanation for the instability of Dutch post-accommodation politics is the nervous, ambivalent, and, as a result, ineffective reaction of the political leaders to such unfamiliar phenomena as the breakdown of bloc cohesion, declining deference, demands for democratization, and political polarization. It started a vicious circle because little was done to deal with these phenomena constructively so that they could grow in an uncontrolled fashion—creating

[17] Robert A. Dahl, *Political Oppositions in Western Democracies* (New Haven: Yale University Press, 1966), p. 400.
[18] See above, pp. 177–179.

even greater problems for the elites. This means that the recent instability of Dutch politics is to an important extent the result of elite behavior fostered during the politics of accommodation when the leaders were "spoiled" because they always had considerable leeway in their relations both with rival bloc leaders and with their own followers.[19] The leaders' failure of will and nerve has also been responsible for the ease with which radical insurgents have taken over established organizations, exemplified by the New Left's capture of the Labor party, the conversion of the V.P.R.O. from a liberal Protestant to a radical left-wing mouthpiece, and the radicalization of the universities with the aid of an extreme university reform law (which, for instance, permits the highest governing organ of the university to have a majority of student and nonacademic personnel representatives) proposed by a weak-kneed minister of education in response to comparatively minor student revolts.[20]

Three developments during the 1960's reinforced the problems of leadership. The strong political personalities of the postwar years all retired in the years around 1960, and their less experienced successors were almost immediately confronted with the first symptoms of the breakdown of the politics of accommodation.[21] At the same time, the growth of television as the most influential channel of political communication suddenly made the weakness and indecisiveness of the new generation of top leaders painfully visible to the public. And among the gravest problems that confronted the new leaders were the controversies surrounding the royal house. The problem of Princess Irene's conversion and marriage was handled fairly well although it left a residue of ill feeling, but the handling of Princess

[19] Daalder, *Politisering en lijdelijkheid in de Nederlandse politiek*, pp. 44–46, 62.

[20] See Daalder, "The Dutch Universities between the 'New Democracy' and the 'New Management,'" *Minerva*, Vol. 12, No. 2 (April 1974), pp. 221–257.

[21] Van den Berg and Molleman, pp. 145–149.

Beatrix's marriage was disastrous. The fact that these royal problems arose in the 1960's was a coincidence, and the monarchy itself can be regarded as an "accident" in the sense that it is not a necessary attribute of a consociational democracy. All three factors, therefore, undoubtedly contributed to the instability of Dutch politics, but it should be emphasized that they were purely coincidental factors, unrelated to the essential characteristics of the transition from consociational to depoliticized democracy—unlike the three explanations given earlier and the two that will be presented below.

(4)   The fourth explanation of the recent political instability in Holland is the country's pure form of proportional representation. Most countries that use this electoral system apply it within districts, thus limiting the chances for very small parties. Only the Netherlands and Israel have countrywide proportional representation. This extreme electoral system has greatly accelerated the breakdown of the politics of accommodation. It has given small groups of dissidents within the established parties the power—in fact, almost a disproportionate power—to exert pressure on their parties' programs and actions because threats of secession have to be taken very seriously. It has also very much strengthened the impact of the new splinter parties. For instance, the electoral success of Democrats '66 in the 1967 election was generally regarded as the most remarkable and significant result of the election; on their first try, they won seven seats in the Second Chamber. However, if a 5 per cent electoral threshold had been in force, as in West Germany, Democrats '66 would have been utterly defeated.[22] And without the 1967 electoral boost, it is very doubtful that they would have grown so rapidly afterwards. It is also worth noting that of the fourteen parties elected to the Second Chamber in 1972 only four received more than 5 per cent of the vote. Proportional representation has thus not only served as an essential element of

[22] See above, pp. 171, 176.

the politics of accommodation but has also considerably hastened its demise.

A SECOND SELF-DENYING PROPHECY?

The last of the five explanations of the post-accommodation political crisis is the profound disagreement among Dutch politicians and activists about how to solve it and how to achieve both greater stability and a better democracy. In Chapter IX, the solution of the multiple crisis in the early years of the twentieth century was explained to a large extent in terms of a self-denying prophecy.[23] It provided the impetus for the transition from a centrifugal to a consociational democracy. Analogously, the recent efforts to democratize Dutch politics, given the increased homogeneity of Dutch society, can be regarded as purposive attempts spurred by a recognition of the inherent instability of the depoliticized type of democracy to effect a transition from depoliticized to centripetal democracy: a new self-denying prophecy (see Figure 2). However, apart from the fact that no widespread consensus on the desirability of fundamental reforms has emerged yet, the big obstacle to a second self-denying prophecy is that there is no consensus among the reformers themselves about the specific methods to be used.

The main disagreement concerns the question of which normative model should be followed—the British or the American. Both British and American democracy, it should be noted, are examples of the centripetal type, but they differ in so many other respects that they do not provide mutually compatible blueprints for reform. The British-style reformers want to give the voters an unambiguous choice between two large parties or, as an approximation of this ideal, between two electoral alliances. Thus, as in the United Kingdom, the voters can decide both which party or alliance receives a

[23] See above, pp. 182–184.

FIGURE 2. THE TWO SELF-DENYING PROPHECIES

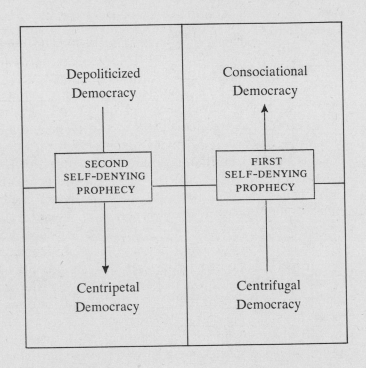

majority in parliament and also who will become prime minister, while at the same time a large and vigorous opposition in the legislature is guaranteed. The "shadow cabinet" of the alliance of the three left-wing parties in 1971 and 1972 was a first important step in this direction.

The alternative, based on the American example, which is preferred by many other reformers, is the introduction of a presidential system, in which the chief executive is elected directly by the voters and in which there is a built-in opposition between the executive and the legislature. Democrats '66 launched this proposal in the form of a "prime minister" directly elected for a fixed term and independent of the confidence of the Second Chamber. They used the term "prime minister" instead of "president" because they did not want to imply that the monarchy should be abolished, but what they had in mind in all other respects was undoubtedly a presidential system. The idea quickly gathered momentum, and a blue-ribbon advisory commission on constitutional reform adopted a somewhat weakened version in its report issued in 1969.[24] What the majority of the commission recommended was the popular election of the cabinet *formateur* who—provided that he had been elected by an absolute majority—would automatically be appointed by the monarch to form a cabinet and who would presumably become the prime minister. In this proposal, parliamentary control over the executive is preserved, but it comes close to a presidential system because it would be very difficult not to appoint a candidate with a large plurality, though not a majority, of the votes and because the Second Chamber would be reluctant to dismiss a prime minister legitimized by popular election.[25] This version of the proposal became part of the program of the three allied left-wing parties in 1971 and 1972 and was formally proposed to the Second Chamber by the Den Uyl cabinet in June 1974.

The chances of fundamental democratic reform have been set back not only by the simultaneous pursuit of incompatible normative models, but also by the fact that the urge to democratize has produced some ill-considered proposals and practices of questionable democratic value. For example, a new rule of the game in Dutch politics appears to be that after the fall of a cabinet, no new cabinet can be formed without "consulting the voters." Accordingly, when the Biesheuvel cabinet fell in the summer of 1972 after one year

[24] *Tweede rapport van de Staatscommissie van advies inzake de Grondwet en de Kieswet* (The Hague: Staatsuitgeverij, 1969), pp. 177–191.

[25] See Lijphart, "Op weg naar een presidentieel stelsel? Opmerkingen over de adviezen van de staatscommissie Cals-Donner," *Socialisme en Democratie*, Vol. 27, No. 3 (March 1970), pp. 140–141.

in office, a new election was called. During the months
before the election and for more than five months afterwards,
while the negotiations for a new cabinet were conducted,
Biesheuvel and most of his ministers remained in office as
caretakers and were thus a government not really subject to
parliamentary control for almost a whole year. Another
example is the insistence of the three left-wing parties that
coalitions and their programs should be formed before instead of after elections. This produced the anomalous situation after the 1972 election when these parties were willing
to form a cabinet with the religious parties but without
changing their own program; the integrity of this program,
somehow sanctified by the fact that it had been submitted to
the voters, was judged more important than the fact that a
clear majority of these voters had failed to support it. Finally,
the conception of the legislator's role as a delegate rather
than a representative has attracted considerable support.
There is nothing undemocratic about this, of course. In the
Labor party, however, there are attempts to enforce this
conception by the establishment of procedures for the recall
of popularly elected officials—a recall to be exercised not
by the voters but by party organs.

Far-reaching reforms appear to be difficult to achieve, but
some minor reforms may succeed in the short run. For instance, slight changes in the electoral system that would limit
the excessive fractionalization of the party system would
represent a distinct improvement. Such a change—the abolition of countrywide proportional representation and the introduction of about twelve districts with at least ten representatives per district—was proposed by the cabinet in June
1974. Public opinion now also favors this change. In the
1954 survey the respondents were very reluctant to change
the electoral system in order to deter small parties, but in
1972 they supported proportional representation within districts by a majority of 51 to 30 per cent.[26] Even such a mild

reform may produce larger, more stable, and more responsible parties and thus pave the way for more fundamental reforms.

The problems of political transition experienced by the Netherlands since about 1967 have been particularly grave because of the rapidity of the breakdown of the politics of accommodation, and proportional representation in its purest form has done a great deal to accelerate it. This is not an entirely negative trait, however. The politics of accommodation does have undeniable flaws, but it is not a regime with a stranglehold on the country it rules. In fact, not the least of the virtues of the politics of accommodation is that it provides the means for its own abolition.

[26] See above, pp. 176–177; and Werkgroep nationaal verkiezings-onderzoek 1972, p. 95.

INDEX

Accommodation: definition of, 103–104, 197, 208–209; establishment of, 104–112, 182–183, 196; institutionalization of, 112–115, 126; after 1917, 115–121; prerequisites for, 188–192; breakdown of, 196–219. *See also* Confederal cooperation; Rules of the game
Action groups, 200–201
Agreement to disagree, 124–125, 130
Algemeen Dagblad, 43, 45, 67
Algemeen Handelsblad, 43, 47, 67
Algeria, 101
Algra, H., 64
Almond, Gabriel A., 9–10, 12, 102, 122 n., 145, 147, 149 n., 150, 153, 192–193, 208
Amendments, 199
Amsberg, Claus von, 86, 201
Andriessen, J. E., 114 n.
Anglo-American political systems, 9, 69, 95, 208. *See also* Great Britain; United States
Anti-Revolutionary party, 23–36 *passim*, 63–64, 67, 125, 140, 142, 202–204, 207–208, 211; and Christian Historical Union, 24, 107, 118–119, 197; and

Socialist labor union, 39; establishment of, 106; and splinter parties, 165–166, 170–176, 206. *See also* Calvinist bloc; Protestant labor union; Reformed Church
Apartheid, 186
April Movement, 72–73, 83
Arbeiderspers, De, 65
Aristotle, 3, 4
Arminians, 17, 83
Assmann, W. P. G., 62
Australia, 19, 21, 22
Austria, 70, 194–195, 208, 212
Authority patterns. *See* Deference
A.V.R.O., 47, 66, 198. *See also* Radio-television associations

Baart, I., 65
Balance of power, 188–189, 191
Banning, W., 39 n.
Beatrix, Princess, 86–88, 201, 213–214
Beaufort, L. J. C., 62
Belgium, 69–70, 84, 97. *See also* Flemings
Bendix, Reinhard, 3
Benthem van den Bergh, Jonkheer G. van, 82 n.

Bentley, Arthur F., 7–8, 13–14,
191–192
Berelson, Bernard R., 193 n.
Berg, J. Th. J. van den, 211 n.,
213 n.
Bernhard, Prince, 86
Beyen, J. W., 117
Biesheuvel, B. W., 127, 207,
217–218
Blocs, 16–23, 23–68 *passim*,
147–148, 154–156, 197–198.
See also Calvinist bloc; Catho-
lic bloc; Liberal bloc; secular
bloc; Socialist bloc
Board of Agriculture, 115
Bogaers, P. C. W. M., 61
Bone, Robert C., 76 n., 119 n.,
183
Borstlap, A., 63
Bouman, P. J., 96 n., 97 n.
Boven, P. M. H. van, 61
Braam, A. van, 91 n., 92
Brabants Nieuwsblad, 62
Breukelaar, A. H. B., 63
Britain. *See* Great Britain
British Commonwealth, 69
Broeksz, J. B., 65
Brogan, D. W., 158
Brouwer, T., 61
Brugmans, I. J., 108 n.
Bruins Slot, J. A. H. J. S., 64
Bruyn, L. P. J. de, 197 n.
Buchanan, William, 21, 22, 23 n.
Burger, J. A. W., 65, 117
Burgomasters, appointment of,
128; election of, 200
Business of politics, 123–124,
134, 191

Cabinet, 113, 126–127, 134–138;
stability of, 75–76, 183, 201
Calhoun, John C., 125
Calvinist bloc, 16–23, 62–64, 79,
83, 210, 211. *See also* Anti-
Revolutionary party; Class
cleavages; Christian Historical

Union; Dutch Reformed
Church; Reformed Church;
Religious cleavages
Canada, 19, 86, 92, 186
Cantril, Hadley, 21, 22, 23 n.
Catholic bloc, 16–23, 61–62, 80–
82, 84–86, 210, 211. *See also*
Catholic Church; Catholic
party; Class cleavages; Re-
ligious cleavages
Catholic Church, 16–17, 60, 62,
66–67, 72–73, 80–81, 204,
210; pastoral letter (1954),
35–36, 39, 41, 94, 112, 158–
159, 198; and Unitas, 39–40;
and patronage, 58; and public
schools, 105–106. *See also*
Catholic bloc; Catholic party;
Church attendance; Irene,
Princess
Catholic labor union, 36–40
passim, 60, 61–62, 109, 197,
210; in Germany, 40. *See also*
Catholic bloc; Catholic
Church; Catholic party
Catholic National party, 24, 165
Catholic party, 23–36 *passim*,
61–62, 67, 140, 178, 197, 198,
208–211; as governing party,
118–121, 189, 204; oligarchy
in, 142–144; and splinter
parties, 164–165, 170–176,
206. *See also* Catholic bloc;
Catholic Church; Catholic
labor union
Catholic People's party. *See*
Catholic party
Central Secretariat for Agriculture and Horticulture, 115
Centrifugal democracy, 209
Centripetal democracy, 209,
215–217. *See also* Pluralism
Christian Democrats, 165, 197,
211
Christian Historical Union, 23–
36 *passim*, 63–64, 67, 140,

Splinter parties, 24, 162–177,
204–207, 214–215
Stapel, J., 157 n.
States-General, 24; relations with
cabinet, 131–133, 134–137,
199, 216–217. *See also* Politi-
cal parties
Stikker, D. U., 115 n.
Structural-functional theory, 7,
9–10
Subcultures. *See* Political sub-
cultures
Suffrage, extension of the, 25,
73, 96, 98, 107–108, 109–112
Summit diplomacy, 112–115,
126–127
Sweden, 19, 100
Switzerland, 92, 212
Syllabus of Errors, 105

Telegraaf, De, 41, 45, 67, 133
Television, 213. *See also* Radio-
television associations
Televizier, 198
Thurlings, Th. L. M., 62, 68
Tijd, De, 41, 45, 60, 62, 67,
85–86
Tocqueville, Alexis de, 5
Toxopeus, E. H., 127
Troelstra, P. J., 74, 84
T.R.O.S., 198. *See also* Radio-
television associations
Trouw, 41, 45, 47, 64, 67, 140
Truman, David B., 8, 11, 12,
13–14, 122 n., 191–192
Two-party systems, 99–100,
215–216

UNESCO survey, 20–23
Unitas, 39–40
United Kingdom. *See* Great
Britain
United States: cleavages in, 8, 9,
11, 19, 21, 22, 23, 69, 194,
208; political stability of, 8, 9,
11, 194, 208, 215–217; and

Vietnam, 101; Marx on, 108;
deference in, 145–147, 149–
154, 192; electoral system of,
170
Universities, 52, 60–68 *passim*,
91, 92, 107, 133, 201, 210,
213
Uyl, J. M. den, 201, 207, 211,
217

Vaderland, Het, 43, 47, 67
Vandenbosch, Amry, 86 n.
V.A.R.A., 47. *See also* Radio-
television associations
Vatican, 210; diplomatic rela-
tions with, 106, 116–117
Verba, Sidney, 12, 14, 102, 104,
122 n., 145, 147, 149 n., 150,
153, 192–193
Vercruijsse, E. V. W., 23 n.
Verkerk, E. P., 63
Vermeulen, W. H., 117 n.
Verplanke, C. J., 39 n.
Verwey-Jonker, H., 91 n.
Vietnam, 101
Vinke, P., 66 n.
Vodopivec, Alexander, 195 n.
Volkskrant, De, 41, 45, 60, 67
V.P.R.O., 48, 210, 213. *See also*
Radio-television associations
Vredeling, H., 65
Vries, C. W., de, 111 n.
Vrije Volk, Het, 41, 43, 45, 59,
65, 67
Vrij Nederland, 47

Waarheid, De, 47
Waerden, C. van der, 65
Walker, Jack L., 192
Waltmans, H. J. G., 81 n.
Warmbrunn, Werner, 47 n.,
86 n., 126 n.
Welderen baron Rengers, W. J.
van, 73 n.
Welter, Ch. J. I. M., 165
West Irian. *See* Decolonization